The Kin Folks

The Kin Folks

FELICIA AGNEW

ISBN: 978-1-960093-14-1   (Paperback)
ISBN: 979-8-89228-488-2   (Hardcover)
ISBN: 978-1-960093-15-8   (eBook)

Printed in the United States of America

Contents

The Kin Folk's

Saturday May 4, 2013 at Church hill Downs

<u>139th Running of the Kentucky Derby</u> – Historic

Attendance: 151,616

<u>Weather:</u> Steady rain all afternoon temperature in the low 60°.

<u>Security:</u> was increased in the aftermath of the Boston Marathon bombing; cooler's and large purses were banned.

<u>The Kentucky Derby</u> is a Grade 1 Stakes race for 3-year thoroughbreds. The distance is one and one quarter miles. (20 horse race)

<u>Rosie Napravnik</u> (Female Jockey) will be riding Mylute in the race. A favorite, odds are 15-1

<u>Kevin Krigger</u> (African American Jockey) will be riding Goldencents; He could become the first African American to win the Kentucky Derby.

Fact: In the races 142 - year history, only women have ever ridden in the Kentucky Derby and the numbers don't get much better when looking at American horse racing as a whole. Overall, Women Make up roughly 10 Percent of professional Jockey's According to the San Diego Tribune. Just 75 of the 750 Jockey's licensed in 2013 were women.

Although the Sport undoubtedly remains a largely male - dominated World, Women Continue to break down barriers as Jockeys, Trainers, Owners, and breeders for the Pioneering Women of horse racing, breaking into the Sport hasn't been easy

In 1968 Us Olympic equestrienne Kathy Kusner became the first licensed Female Jockey after she sued the Maryland Racing Commission for denying her application for a Jockey's license on the base of gender.

Toward the end of 1968. Penny Ann Farly who had been granted a Jockeys license shortly after Kusner, was denied the chance to become the first Looman to Compete in the Kentucky Derby. When the Male Jockeys boycotted the race to keep her from participating.

Patricia Cooksey, she's the 2nd Women to ride in the Kentucky Derby. Marked another major milestone for Women riders when she became the first female Jockey to compete in the Preakness in 1985 while riding Tajawa.

In 1993, Julie Krone won the Belmont stakes, making her the first female Jockey to win a Triple Crown race. She would later go on to become the first woman to be inducted into the National Museum of Racing Hall of fame in 2000.

Since 1977, Female Jockeys have been allowed in the Grand National horse race following the passing of the Sex Discrimination Act 1975. A total of 19 Female Jockeys have entered the Grand National. Since then Charlotte Brew on her horse, Barony Fort, was the first woman to compete in the race in 1977.

Rachael Blackmore became the first female. Jockey to win the Grand National winning the 2021 race aboard Minella Times.

In 1988 female participation was at an all - high, As 3 women entered for the first time. None of their horses made the finish.

In 2012, the first female jockey to finish in the top 3 was Katie Walsh on Sea bass.

Rosie Napravnik: A 25 year old Female Jockey, Trail blazer, Pioneer, and extra Ordinary talents. One of the World's best Jockey's. She could be the first female to win the Kentucky Derby in the 139th year history of the race. A lean mean, riding Machine, and not a push over.

Napravnik was exposed to horses from a young age - her father worked as a Farrier, while her mother trained event ponies. She stumbled across an old VHS video. It inspired her to win a Triple Crown race. At 7 years - old she followed her sister into Pony racing for wanna be Jockey's. By age 14 she was working as an apprentice Jockey, which gave her the foundation for horsemanship.

She began her riding career pimlico Race Course in Baltimore, MD. In 2005, she was the first Female to ever win the Kentucky Oaks. She's a gentle giant but, for a Female Jockey it's a bit harder to get yourself established. Rosie is the fifth - highest earning Jockey on the Circuit today. Last year amassing a fortune of more than $ 12.4 million in Prize money, she's 3rd Overall in terms of races won. In 2012, her horses finished in the top three in nearly half the races she entered.

My lute lost to Revolutionary by less than a length in the 2013 Preakness. This will be her Second time riding him, "she says" Judge me on my talent, not my sex. And she's not afraid of a sloppy track with mud in her face. Mylute is gonna be live shot, layed back and not bothered by much. Rosie has great dedication but she suffered five major accidents and taken a total of 15 months of work due to injuries but that's a part of the job.

A typical day involves waking up at 5 a.m. competing in up to 12 races late into the evening, then she will have a meal. Pressure is always put on Jockeys to meet strick weight restrictions.

It could be difficult balancing a grueling career and social life. Once she finishes smashing the record books, Napravnik hopes to pursue another dream starting a family. "My husband and I are very excited about having a family.

"It's a stereotype to say that all female riders are finesse riders. A lot are, but there are also men that have that finesse factor as well."

She's the first woman to win two Breeders Cups. She won the 2012 Breeders Cup Juvenile period and the 2014 Breeders Cup Distaff after her 2014 when she retired from horse racing revealing she was 6 weeks pregnant she won a total of 1,877 starts.

She continues to assist her husband Joe sharp with training horses. She has even competed in eventing with an OTTB (of the track thoroughbred) she's now an advocate for repurposing OTTB's giving them new careers.

Kevin Krigger - If successful, the 29 year old from the Virgin Islands will be the first black man to win the title since 1902. Regardless he'll be the first African-American rider to compete since Marlon Julian in 2000 who finished 7th aboard Curule.

Still chasing his dream "I've never given up on it." Horses were a part of his life for the rural community and as a four-year-old Krigger would pull the animals next to cars so he could climb on board. At 10 years old he was given his first mare challenging other children two races on the beach and down the dirt roads. He would even balance his saddle on the arm of mama's sofa and pretend to ride it.

At age 17 he headed to the U.S to follow his dream. He had some failures, in 2011 he found his stride, winning 124 races and notching up to $2.8 million in prize money. He got a call from his agent Tom Knust, to compete at some of the top Southern California Circuits. He packed up his girlfriend and four children and moved to Seattle. He came under Kentucky Derby trainer Doug O'Neil with a chance to ride the horse of his dreams Goldencents (A favorite)

"Krigger said, his riding style is patience uncanny sense of peace and supreme self-confidence. Goldencents has a quick burst of early speed and a favorable post position. He can run all day he scored his first Grade 1 Victory just last month when Goldencents won the Santa Anita Derby. He's been made keenly aware of the history of black Jockeys in the Derby. He keeps a photo of Jimmy Winkfield in his locker he brought along to Churchill Downs for good luck.

In 2013, Krigger is one of 50 black Jockeys competing in the U.S out of an estimated 1,000. "I would love to see maybe in 5 years, 10 years from now we have African-American riders in every (Jockey) Colony he said."

A sport now dominated by Jockeys from Latin America. I'm effective on a horse that wants to win. No matter how much a person love a horse, he must have great chemistry with a horse.

He rises at 5 am each morning – and success will have nothing to do with his skin color. We have to earn the respect of our trainers. "The next black Jockey isn't going to ride in the Kentucky Derby because of me - He's gotta go get it.

He's been the regular rider for Goldencents and 4 of 6 races. One of Goldencents owners is Louisville Basketball Coach Rick Pitino, who has a 5 percent share in the colt.

He will have about 30 friends and family - including his Fiancee and his four children ages 2 to 11 cheering him on Saturday.

Horse Racing Industry:

The amount of money contributed to the United States Government by Horse Racing Industry is an incredible amount. On average the sport produces 38.8 billion dollars, of which whopping $1.88 billion is paid in annual taxes. The amount goes to the United States. Europe makes an average about 45.3 billion United States dollars. Then, when taking into account supplies and employees they produced around 101.6 billion US dollars.

Governments around the globe benefit highly from the industry, and horse racing being banned could have a drastic effect on entire populations from lack of money. It could also cost millions of people around the globe their jobs and businesses. According to a recent labor poll over 4.6 million people are involved in the horse racing industry in some way, with other owners, employees, service providers, or volunteers. This include 2,000,000 horse owners of which 238,000 are involved in breeding.

When it comes to competing such as the Jockeys and handlers 481 OHD people are involved. In other activities such as grooms, veterinarians, and caretakers, 1.1 million involved. 119,000 Service Providers, and 702,000 employees, full-and Part-time and 2 million family members and volunteers. This mean that 1 out of every 63 Americans is involved with horses. Many of these jobs are held by lower-income families. Banning the horse racing industry could affect the local areas around them bad. The results of the study done by students at the University of Louisville, show that the horse business is highly diverse industry. It supports a wide variety of activities in all regions of the country. Primarily, rural activities of breeding, training, maintaining, and riding horses with some more urban activities of operating race tracks, off-track betting parlors horse shows and public sales.

These strip mall shops gain money and business from these enthused shoppers. If there is no race track, these shops and small businesses could have a plummet in sales and be shut down for the lack of ability to pay. Having the tracks removed could lower business income for hospitals schools as well as universities. The United States alone produces 3 billion from horse racing and tourism. Over 67% of activity and gambling money come from tourists going and paying at the race track. As a source of entertainment, food venues, and shopping areas round the premises of the track. An ideal hot spot for tourists to spend their money.

Danger's of Horse Racing:

Horse racing is very dangerous sport, and can result <u>in broken bones, concussions brain damage and even paralysis</u>. Jockeys are often thrown off their horses and the horse has a potential of landing on a Jockeys. A horse outweighs a Jockey by almost 1000 pounds and a Jockey can risk death resulting from a fall. Especially if they are weak due to eating disorder such as anorexia nervosa, eating disorders can result in weakened skeleton and can result in chapter bones that otherwise wouldn't be broken.

<u>Jose Espinoza</u> = an American Jockey from Mexico City, Mexico. 2013 was his first Kentucky derby. He rode giant finish and come in 10th place. In August 2013 Espinoza suffered a traumatic brain injury at Saratoga Race Course in New York. He was thrown from a mount after crossing the finish line. Rajiv Maragh was riding behind him and fell also. Maragh got out immediately: Espinoza lay motionless for several minutes while being attended too. He was pretty banged up.

<u>May 14, 2007</u> - Jose was injured in a racing accident at Belmont park. He suffered a dislocated ankle with the multiple fractures, which required surgery and he would be out for 6 months.

<u>May 3, 2014</u> - Jose found it difficult to talk about horses, following a physically devastating accident more than 8 months ago at Saratoga. Espinoza is just now accepting the fact that barring a miracle he will never ride competitively again, and it would be dangerous and maybe lead to death if he fell again. He didn't know if he would get his passion back for horse racing. He figured he could live his dream out through younger brother Victor Espinoza. He's a triple crown winning Jockey. Victor will be riding California Chrome in the Kentucky Derby.

Jose says he has good and bad days, but wants to attend the Derby. He added if he goes it would be a last minute decision.

Espinoza perked up when asked what seeing his brother win the Derby would mean to him. "Oh man, I'm going to feel great, he said." That's going to be my medicine, my every thing."

Horse racing Terms / Jockey's

Horse racing is one of the biggest and wealthiest sports on the planet. It can be a little complicated for many with its numerous terminologies from filler to <u>Ginneas</u>, to <u>Furlongs</u>, <u>Gelding</u>, <u>Fractions</u>, <u>Quarter Track</u>, <u>Quarter Pole</u>, <u>Rank</u>, <u>Lug in</u>, <u>Rate</u>, <u>Scratch</u>, <u>odds</u>, <u>Shake up</u>, <u>Turf Course</u>, and <u>many more</u>.

Somehow with the advancement in technology, the introduction of Artificial Synthetic and all-weather tracks is now been installed at race courses across the world.

Jockey's:

To qualify for the program aspiring Jockeys must have a (High School diploma or Ged) and experience riding and training horses. It's not mandatory to attend and graduate from NARA to become a Jockey. An aspiring Jockey can apply Jockey apprenticeship license at the age of 16, in most states.

There's 5 essential requirements they must meet to be eligible to race. (Weigh in) Professional Jockeys must meet strict weight restrictions to be able to ride, having to adhere to a minimum riding weight for a particular phrase or face disqualification...

(1) Weigh in = must meet strict weight restrictions to ride. May take months of preparation to ensure they come in under weight.

(2) Fitness = must be able to control a fast-moving horse. They are professional athletes and need to be extremely fit and healthy. Must have the right strength and endurance to control the horse while racing. There's a variety of tests including cardiovascular and strength with a focus on upper and lower body. Core strength.

(3) Tack up = you must be a very good rider with horsemanship skills.

(4) Warm up and Control = you and your horse should warm up before exercise, to prevent injury. Must be able to control a horse running 40 mph. The weight of jockey ranges from 108 to 118 LB, including Jockeys equipment.

(5) Riding Assessment = Jockey's must be avid riders but handling a thoroughbred can be a challenge. Jockeys must have the ability to gallop at least six furlongs at one time. They must be able to demonstrate they can monitor pace and control a race horse according to the assessor's instruction.

($\star$) The Salaries of Horse Jockeys: In the USA range from $10,039 to $271,427 with a medium salary of $48,880.

The middle 57% of Horse Jockeys makes between $48,882 and $123,036 with the top 86% making $271,427.

Horse Racing Terms:

Bug Boy: An Apprentice Jockey

Jockey Agent: An individual that obtains rides for a Jockey.

Fractions: Clocking at every quarter-mild increments in either a race or work out.

Furlong: An eight of a mile.

Quarter Crack: An injury to the hoof of the horse.

Quarter Pole: Post on the infield rail that indicates 2 furlongs to the finish line.

Scratch: To withdraw a horse in a race.

Sloppy Track: A wet track covered with puddles, but not yet "muddy".

Handicap: Added weight to an adept runner to equalized the playing field.

Off The Pace: A horse that is lagging a little in the beginning of the race.

Pace: The speed of the leading runners in a race.

Post: Another name for starting gate.

Closer: A horse running better in the later part of the race than the beginning.

Turf Course: A grass covered course.

Mudder: A horse that races well on muddy tracks.

Lug In: a horse (drift toward the rail) in during the stretch run.

Odds: a horse winning a race based upon the pari-mutuel bets of betting public.

Pace setter: the horse that is running in front (on the lead).

Exacta: a players bet attempts to pick the 1st and 2nd place horse on one ticket.

Back Stretch: the straight way on the far side of the track.

Co- Favorites: when 3 or more selections share status as a Favorite (have lowest odds)

Favorite: It has the most likely chance of winning the race.

Superfecta: A bet placed on 4 horses to cross finish line in exact chosen order.

Rail runner: Horse that prefers to run next to the inside rail.

Long shot: Given a little chance at winning.

Stretch Runner: Horse that runs its fastest nearing the finish of the race.

3 Triple Crown Races:

The Triple Crown= a series of 3 thoroughbred races each spring at different <u>tracks and distances</u> over the course of 5 weeks.

- It's open to 3 year old Thoroughbred, which means each horse has only one shot to win it in his or her lifetime.

- In American horse racing championship attributed to a 3-year old thoroughbred that in a single season wins the Kentucky Derby, the Preakness Stakes, and the Belmont Stakes.

- Each horse must be nominated which includes a fee, before running. Usually that happens in late winter, but sometimes it's done just days before the race, in which case the fee increases greatly.

- A Triple Crown Winning horse earns the winners share of the purse for each of 3 races a horse must sweep all 3 races.

Kentucky Derby = $1.86 billion

Preakness = $900,000

Belmont = $800,000 and a Silver Trophy plus having your horses name forever etched in the History books.

<u>Kentucky Derby:</u> the first race of the triple crown is 1 1/4 mile long. It may be the first time the horse's race over that distance, but it likely won't be the last. 1 and 1/4 miles is the standard classic distance. A few other races are the same length, The Breeders Cup Classic, Travers Stakes, and Santa Anita Handicap. The Kentucky Derby is also known as "Run For The Roses".

<u>The Preakness:</u> usually two weeks later. The Middle Jewel of the Triple Crown is a slightly shorter 1 3/16 miles.

The race is in no way a push over. But it lacks the atmosphere of the Derby or the challenges of the Belmont. So it has been the easiest to win in recent years. It's held on a Dirt Track at Pilmico Race Course in Baltimore, Maryland.

Often called "The run for the Black-eye Susans / "The Second Jewel" or Middle Jewel" of the Triple Crown.

Belmont Stakes: The final race the Victory required to Win the Triple Crown, is the ultimate test. At 1 1/2 miles, it's the longest race that many of these horses will ever run. This challenge makes it unique and it has proven the most elusive of the Triple Crown Jewels. In the 37 years between Affirmed in 1978 and American Pharoah in 2015, 13 horses won the Derby and Preakness but not the Belmont Stakes. It's held 3 weeks after the Preakness at Belmont Park in Belmont, New York. Just East of New York City.

Triple Crown Winner's

Year	Winner	Jockey	Trainer	Owner	Breeder
1973	Secretariat	Ron Turcotte	Lucien Laurin	Penny Chenery	Penny Chenery
1978	Affirmed	Steve Cauthen	Laz Barrera	Harbor View Farm	Harbor View Farm
2015	American / Pharoah	Victor Espinoze	Bob Baffert	Ahmed Zayat	Ahmed Zayat
2018	Jestify	Mike & Smith	Bob Baffert	Winstar Farm, et al.	John D. Gunther

Road To The Kentucky Derby

The Kentucky Derby is set up by a point system which features 34 stakes for two and three-year-old Thoroughbreds. The point system replaces the previous system which consisted of about 185 graded stakes races worldwide. The series is divided into two phases, The Kentucky Derby Prep Season and The Kentucky Derby Championship Season. The Prep Season consists of 17 races on dirt or synthetic surfaces over distances of at least 1-mile that typically are run between late September and late February. Points are awarded to the top 4 finishers in each race on a 10-4-2-1 scale. The Championship Season consists of 2 legs and a Wild Card round. The first leg incudes 8 races with a 50-20-10-5 scale. The second leg includes 7 races with a 100-40-20 scale. The Wild Card consists of one race and has a 10-4-2-1 scale.

The Top 20 point earners can earn a spot in the Kentucky Derby Starting Gate if at least 20 horses enter the race. Up to 24 horses may enter the race and 4 horses can be listed as also eligible and would be ranked in order accordingly in case any horses be scratched prior to the race. If 2 or more horses have the same number of points, the tie breaker to get into the race will be earning in non-restricted stakes races, whether or not they are graded.

-The Kentucky Derby requires a horse to unleash a top Physical Performance, during what will certainly be one of the grueling and taxing races in a Colts Career.

-As a result, the months leading up to the Derby Provided the foundation on which a winning Performance is based.

-The goal of any top class trainer is to condition his horse to perform at it's best on the big day-not two or three, or four weeks early.

The Jockey Club: An organization dedicated to the improvement of Thoroughbred breeding and pacing. Incorporated Feb. 10, 1894 in

New York City, The Club Services as North Americans Thoroughbred registry, responsible, for the maintenance of "The America's Stud Book", a registry of all Thoroughbred foaled in the United States, Puerto Rico, and Canada; and of all Thoroughbreds imported into those countries from Jurisdictions that have a registry recognized by The Jockey Club and the International Stud Book Committee.

The Kin Folks

Mama Faye: Grow up in Athens Georgia. She's in her late 70s she loves gardening and cooking. She's a widow. She has a son named Frederick, mama always had a love for Horses and Sports. Some of the town's people call her Sports Mom. She loves people and putting together Social Functions.

Mama still have Dreams and Visions. She love watching all of Tyler Perry movies. Mama is the glue to this family and Community. There's never a dull moment around her. These are a few jobs she's done. Grey Hound bus driver and she still have a current CDL license. Limo for the funeral Home, grave digger operating heavy equipment. Handy women, undertaker, construction and electrician. Sometimes a mid-wife when called upon.

Mama can fix anything under a hood. This is why these people respect her so much. She always have the answers.

Chapter 1

To start Faye Wilson (Mama Faye) just got home from a long day of shopping. Her vibrant personality. Everyone loves her long silvery hair down her back. Mama's always been an extrovert, and putting people before herself. A die heart Sports Mom. She needs something to look forward to that doesn't come in a bottle mamas been thinking for a long time about having this Kentucky Derby party. She feels it would help her cope more with her grieving. She miss the socializating part in her life. She's always been a giver.

Her dream is to reach her long term goal. A reality show and to build a Track Side Training Center for thoroughbreds and 2nd a horse therapy stable for special needs children, and families on her 20 acre's of land. That was left to her by her late husband Robert who died tragically 6 years ago. He was a long-haul trucker and was hit head on by a dump truck. The whole town was devastated hearing the news.

Mama still get's shaky feeling the hurt and pain. Mama's dark skinned with high cheek bones. Her father was a farmer and her mom a school teacher. Mama is the Jack of all trades.

People assumed that...she was crazy because of her skills. Her love for horses started in her childhood. She had a job grooming and training horses as a teenager. She's been a pillar and activist for her community.

Her husband left her a huge 2-story brick house. It has 5 bedrooms cathedral ceilings, storm shelter built in the basement. It sits in the heart of Athens, Georgia, Beautiful climbing rose bushes, Japanese maples and plenty bird houses. Athens, Georgia is a college town known for it's peaches and peanuts, and football, Georgia Tech & Georgia Bull Dogs.

Fred Wilson is mama's only child, sophomore in high school. He's 6'3" with, medium complexion and short dreads. Energetic, and zits popping everywhere on his face. He's sneaky, always curious, and can tell a lie faster than a dog can lick a plate." Wrestling is his dream.

He think he's the "rock" because his bow-legged and a 6 pack. Mama have 3 brothers and 2 sister's. Uncle Bubba (Grill Master), Aunt Peaches (Party Animal), Eugene (King Pin/Drug Dealer) Did 20 years in prison. Lottie (The Lottery Winner years ago.)

Thurs Afternoon.
It's mid-afternoon at mama's house. There's a band of heavy cloud, somewhat of a storm brewing. But, there's a lively feel there. Fred just walked in from school. Woah! Fred jaw drops; this place is stunning, superb, and splendid. You put this together? Mama answered, you know I did Tupperware parties, and a few creations of my own.

A mint Julep and Bourbon Bar? It's the traditional beverage of Churchhills Down. He walks to the Sun room, buffet style dinner tables with a run for the roses centerpiece. Derby games, banners everywhere Mama made tee-shirts for the guest.
Womens - Talk Derby Too ME. (yellow)
Men - When Does A Horse Talk? Whinny feels like it! (Brown)
Mama, I'm so proud of you. This party gonna be on and popping.

Oh! Wait we have a menu: Amish Peanut Butter Pie.

And some unmentionables. Mennonite soft white cookies.

In addition we will have other foods. Saturdays gonna be busy. So I need your help. He replied sure it's done. Mama checked it off her list. Mama's feeling a little tired and jittery. She's been off her daily routine, Imma take care of that shortly. She hugged herself and took a break.

Mama hates going to the doctor, she's been using her natural remedies Forever, especially for her aches and pains.

Her first remedy is 1/4 cup of yellow Root Tea. If that don't work she goes to her signature remedy three tablespoons of moonshine straight down the throat. She keeps a reserve jar in her curio cabinet at all times.

Mama is the only one that can get moonshine boys outta the woods. When she have a function they flock to it and she get a chance to sample sum of their flavors like grapes, peaches, strawberries, and muscadines. So she's convinced it's a medicine not an addiction. After testing the flavors Charles and Henry asked for her tweaks and math for the perfect adjustments.

Chapter 2

<u>Friday Early Morning</u>
Mama said, as far as I know this rain should be slacking up shortly. Mama's been up cooking all night. Fred is still helping unload and make the ladies comfortable. Betty drove from Mississippi, she's Uncle Bubba's secret crush. Fred said, "Uhh! You making them Jamician Hot Wing's and Mississippi Sin Dip? Of course, I heard you loved them wings. Hahaha!

<u>Friday Evening</u>
Lottie took all of the ladies on a shopping spree. Mama stayed home to finish baking cakes. Fred's in his room laying down parlay in (chilling) "He thought, Betty is real fresh, I see the lust in her eyes."

Ughh! She might be too much for Bubba. Nah! He's a O.G. (old gangster) when the ladies get back its movies and cooking. Mama pulled out the wines.

At the present rain is expected the whole weekend in Kentucky. Some horses love the sloppy track, some wet dirt is thrown in their faces.

Just like pro athletes, jockeys all have their habits. Some like to push their mounts to get the lead. While others refuse to give ground on turns. Some jockeys are great with leading speed horses and others prefer to ride come from behind horses. Some are great turf riders and not so good on the dirt. Mama said, see they have problems just like we do.

In addition Peaches is running late. Mama is irate. She will be late for her own funeral. Listen. Them "Bald spots on " the side of her head is like a lie, the bigger it gets the harder it is to cover up." Mama shouted down stairs, Fred keep an eye on the oven bell. Fred ain't heard nothing. She belt up the steps to get a sip. Mama started day dreaming and it turned into a cat-nap.

The oven bell is ringing like crazy. Fred is upset with Belinda his girl, arguing on the phone. Cookie his cat wants attention, won't stop whinning. Fred throws her against the wall, she runs to Shorty's house. She found about his hook up on social media and broke-up with him. He's stuttering and sweating, begging on his knees. She hung up. He choked.

Peaches is ringing the doorbell; Fred is upstairs, can't even find the oven bell. Oh my! What's burning? Fred said, mama's pound cakes. Where's the fire extinguisher? Peaches stomped her feet, where's Faye? Fred replied, upstairs day dreaming. You'll didn't hear the oven bell ringing like Crazy? Fred replied Nah! I was in a heated conversation with Belinda.

The whole kitchen is ablaze. Fred opened all windows and doors to let the smoke escape. Peaches peeked in the oven, and took out the cakes all 3 burned on the bottom. Who's gonna eat these? Faye be doin too much! Fred agreed, "I feel you auntee!"

Mama creeping down the stairs, what's going on? Why do my kitchen smell like a burning forest fire!

Mama seen the cakes this was heartbreaking. I've never burned a cake in my life. Peaches commented, why didn't you turn off the oven?

I got side tracked, waiting on you. But I know how to fix them, Peaches blurted, if you cut the bottom off, it will still taste burnt. It will only take 10 minutes. Peache's said something else smart. Mama balled her fisk up, bout to hit Peaches. She aimed for that ball spot, on the side of her head. Fred jumped in between them, calm down mama! You know your "sewing machine's outta thread" What sewing machine? I gave up sewing 3 years ago. It's a Joke mama. Haha!

Fool! You trying to call me crazy? Imma lay you down. "You getting too big for your britches", "It's A Wrap!" The kitchen is "Quiet as a church mouse!" Peaches is making her speciality BBQ chicken feet, and Fred hate the smell. (foul)

Fred hightail downstairs to get his car keys and some condoms. Upon opening the door he got a big surprise. He shouted! Yo! Cookie why did you urinate all over my pillows? He looked under the bed, Cookie's gone. Mama told Fred to go check on Bubba and come straight back.

Don't be over there watching wrestling. You're already addicted to it. Mama you're the one who got me hooked since 2 years old...you knew that's my dream to become a professional wrestler. Fred! You just want someone to stroke your ego and recite scripts for the show. He had a vacant look.

Fred coughed! Mama why was dad always throwing college down my throat? Because he didn't want you to be a thug. He wasn't all that squeaky clean either. Whatcha mean? He mumbled under his breath. I heard he had outside kids. What did you say? Ugh! Nothing "That was my inner voice. You need to fix that."

Fred said, here's the list of Derby Contenders. Looks like we have a lot of favorites this year. Who you got mama? I'm going with Mylute. A young women Jockey Rosie will be riding him. She has experience and she's familiar with the horse. Plus I want to see her make history.

Before ending the conversation, something popped into mama's head. She told Fred about how cruel Diane Crump was treated in 1969. The Pari-mutuel race was so controversial that she needed a police escort at the event. She told a reporter and CNN. "There were cat-calls" "[People said]" go home, cook dinner, you need to go to the kitchen, you don't need to be out here getting other Jockey's Killed"

Fred said, Wild! Mama that's heartbreaking. She said, oh! Yeah! And I had my share of discrimination also, especially when I drove the dump Truck and the Grey Hound Bus. But you have to move on and enjoy life and treat everybody right inspite of the pain.

And for some reason, I'm really pulling for Rosie Napravnik. She looks like a history maker.

2013 Kentucky Derby: (Contenders)

Horse Name	Post	Last Race	Odds
Verrazano	14	Won Wood Memorial	4–1
Orb	16	Won Florida Derby	7–2
Goldencents	8	W– San Anita Derby	5–1
Java's War	19	W– Blue Grass	15–1
Overanalyze	9	W– Arkansas Derby	15–1
Revolutionary	3	W– Louisiana Derby	10–1
Line of Battle	11		30–1
VY Jack	20	3rd in Wood Memorial	15–1
Will Take Charge	17	Won Rebel Stakes	20–1
It's My Lucky Day	12	2nd in Florida Derby	15–1
Palace Malice	10	2nd in Blue Grass S.	20–1
Normandy Invasion	5	2nd in Wood Memorial	12–1
Frac Daddy	18	2nd in Arkansas D.	50–1
Mylute	6	2nd in Louisiana D.	15–1
Oxbow	2	5th in Arkansas D.	30–1
Falling Sky	13	4th in Arkansas D.	50–1
Charming Kitten	15	3rd in Blue Grass S.	20–1
Golden Soul	4	4th in Louisiana D.	50–1
Giant Finish	7	3rd in Spiral Stakes	50–1

A few of the Picks:
Fred – Golden Soul
Shorty – Revolutionary
Uncle Bubba – Verrazano
Mama Faye – Mylute

2013 Kentucky Derby Post Positions
Jockey's / Trainer's

Post	Horse	Jockey	Trainer	Odds
1	Black Onyx	Joe Brave	Kelly Breen	50-1
2	Oxbow	Gary Stevens	D. Wayne Lukas	30-1
3	Revolutionary	Calvin Borel	Todd Pletcher	10-1
4	Golden Soul	Robby Albarado	Dallas Stewart	50-1
5	Normandy Invasion	Javier Costellano	Chad Brown	12-1
6	Mylute	Rosie Napravnick	Tom Amoss	15-1
7	Giant Finish	Jose L. Espinoza	Antony W. Dutrow	50-1
8	Goldencents	Kevin Krigger	Doug O'Niell	5-1
9	Overanalyz	Rafael Bejarano	Todd Pletcher	15-1
10	Palace Malice	Mike Smith	Todd Pletcher	20-1
11	Line of Battle	Ryan Moore	Aiden O'Bien	30-1
12	It's My Lucky Day	Elvis Trujillo	Eddie Pies, Jr.	15-1
13	Falling Sky	Luis Saez	John Terranova II	50-1
14	Verrazano	John R. Velazquez	Tod Pletcher	4-1
15	Charming Kitten	Edgar Prado	Tod Pletcher	20-1
16	Orb	Joel Rosario	Claude R. MC Gaughey III	7-2 (favorite)
17	Will Take Charge	Jon Court	D. Wayne Lukas	20-1
18	Frac Daddy	Victor Lebron	Kenny MC Peek	50-1
19	Java's War	Julien Leparoux	Kenny MC Peek	15-1
20	Vyjack	Garret Gomez	Rudy Rodriguez	15-1

Chapter 3

Previously, Fred's car wouldn't start. He's in the driveway. Jumped into his Volkswagon Gulf. Snaps!

I thought mama fixed my alternator, maybe I will fondle it. He took a glimpse under the hood.

Someone's been under my hood. My spark plugs are missing. Suddenly he was attacked by a swarm of bees. He shouted help! And dashed back into the car. Wild! That was a close call.

I believe that mama been playing with my hood. Disconnecting parts under my hood. She know I like to roll. He's texting Shorty for a ride. While sitting in the car; he decided to check-out the derby horse list.

Woah! These some weird horse names. I gotta choose one that can handle the stretch and far turn. I'm looking for a closer, a dare-devil. For me that would be golden soul. He's a threat to make the late charge.

Shorty is Fred's neighbor, Fred's best friend. He grew up Amish/Mennonite. And trying to transition into the real world. At 15 he was baptized by sprinkling. Black is his favorite color. He's been farming and caring for animal's most of his life.

Shorty just pulled up, what's up cuzz? Everything! Cookie ran away from home. Nah! She been sleeping on my porch, she was acting nervous and didn't want to play. Fred said, she'll be alright. You know cats have nine lives man. Right! Fred whispered, it's Friday night let's go and hit the club. Shorty nodded, let's go hit Da Club. See my slang is better. Fred just for a little while, I need to get you to Uncle Bubba. Shorty have you checked out the horses? Yeah! It's 2 favorites. Orb and Verrazano. I'm going with Revolutionary, hot potato coming off 3 straight victories.

Shorty said, I can't wait to attend Jockey School. I gotta keep my weight down. And your hygiene too. Huh! Never mind, bruh you only 100 pounds. They laughed.

At present, just turned into "The Hole in The Wall (Club)." There's a lively feel to it. Action, flashing lights. Small white building with paint chipping off. Limited seating and parking. Crickets are very loud, lightening bugs are out too. Since were underage, Fred paid Big Terry (The Bouncer) twenty buck's to let us in. Upon walking in, we could feel the energy in the building.

Therefore it's getting late, Fred is lit! Shorty's been trying to steer him out since 11:30 pm. He wants to make it rain. Shorty went over to Dmark a school friend, and told him to drop Fred off. He agreed. At 1:00 am Dmark tried to get Fred home. He's got a ride already.

Meanwhile, mama's been blowing up Fred and Bubba's phone. Bubba hinted, I told you that boy is getting too grown. Now he's, outta control. Send him to me and I will handle him. Since he want to become a wrestler. I need to put him in one of my headlocks. Mama hung up! She thought to herself, nah! That idiot gonna kill my baby.

Thirdly, Shorty had a lot on his mind driving. He needed more information on this club.

Uncle Bubba is old school. Quick tempered, and in denial. Everyone hates when he pulls out that pipe. He's 3 yrs. older than Mama Faye. He's a grill master at heart tho. Right on!

Now, its 2:00 am Fred hooked up with this stripper Coco after making it rain. He could barely stand up. Coco took him to the Motel 8. He paid for everything. This was one wild night.

Saturday 6:30 am Fred woke up! Nacked as a Jay bird and handcuffed to the bed. Also a bull whip on the nightstand. Scratches all over his back. He was helpless until 11am when cleaning service entered. Crystal's mouth went wide open! Ahem! What happened to you? Lady can you get management to uncuff me? I will be right back.

Mr. Price bounced over there with bolt cutters. He laughed in hysterics. What kinda hook up was this? Craigs list! Are you sure it was a she?

Yes sir, "My wallet please!" Argh!..this wallet is empty. My $200.00 gone down the drain." Mr. Price busted out laughing again. "Son you missed your calling!" Wish I could've watch this movie with some popcorn. Hahaha!

Shorty just pulled up, laying on that horn. Fred jetted out the room. Glad to see you. Last night was crabby dogg. How you get handcuffed to the bed? That had to be wicked. Fred said, I was lit. We smoked some high grade weed it was game over for me. I don't remember anything. I was trying to protect you. You had to make it rain. Hahaha! You're one crazy dude.

Mama is irate, she even blew my phone up. Is that a fact? Hopefully she's calm by now. Now I gotta face Uncle Bubba. That was my horse betting money. Crap! Looks like she stole my phone too. I thought you love Berlinda? I do but I guess I got a little dog in me. It runs in the family; as he continued pushing his tongue inside his cheek.

Shorty said, sound like you got Hood Wink Bruh! Ughhh! You might be right! They both laughed. Hey! Shorty I see your slang is increasing, yeah! But I gotta be careful around the Priest. I use my words very carefully when he's present, because he might turn into a goon, Fred said Darn!

By the way Shorty when is your dad gonna get rid of that Porta-Potty on the side of your house? You'll have two bathrooms inside the house. Somebody need to let the priest know that's unnecessary. Shorty said, he doesn't get it. He did the same thing when we lived in Ohio. It's a family Tradition, yikes!

Fred said, he might need to get checked out. Shorty stated, by who? The Priest is sick in the head! That's why I'm going to Jockey school, my meal ticket out. He needs to breed his own animals, I'm no Veterinarian. Fred couldn't stop laughing I feel you cuzz! I would do the same thing. Shorty said, my Pop's got serious mental issues, He wants to hide behind the cloth and call the shots! Shorty thought sometimes I wonder if He's right with God himself?

Chapter 4

<u>Early Sat. Morning</u>

Bubba's been up since 5:00 am. There's a mist rolling in, a light wind off and on. Bubba's been up all night putting his, top of the line, <u>Pit Boss Grill</u> together 11 – in one, $747.00 Features: <u>Grill</u>, <u>Sear</u>, <u>Bake</u>, <u>Stirfry</u>, <u>Char-grill</u>, <u>Smoke</u>, <u>Braises</u>, <u>Roast</u>, <u>Scramble</u>, <u>BBQ</u>, and <u>Saute</u>. Weather will be cloudy 60° very humid today.

Weather don't bother Bubba. He says a grill master knows how to cook in any type of climate. He puts 7 slabs pork spare ribs on charcoal side, 6 baby back on the smoker side. Louisiana bake beans in the cast iron skillet. Cajun corn and Sweetheat Southern Glazed Salmon.

Fred is dropped off at Uncle Bubba's. Boy where you been all night? It's a long story, I will tell you when I wake up. I feel crummy, Bubba said, "You look like a dummy." Hahaha! But, before Fred close his eyes. He thought, "I hope Bubba don't jack his new grill up. It would be a national disaster.

Bubba have the grill on the grass in the front yard. He's sitting on his wrap around porch. Everything is cooking good. There's a sweet and zesty aroma in the air. The wind is picking up more. Bubba set his speakers on his porch, put on some blues music. Some of his favorite artist are BB King, Muddy Waters, Blind Boy Fuller, and Johnny Lee Hooker.

He smoking a cigar and notice a few crows and black birds flying over his house. He thought, ain't nothing dead around here. Right on! The wind have picked up to 30mph.

The new grill and blues music is relaxing Bubba. He starting to nod but keep's fighting it off. He's popping his neck. He drops the oven mitt in his hand. 3 minutes later he drops the meat fork and goes out like a light. Something is burning, smelling horrible all through the neighborhood. A screeching sound then a loud boom like an explosion. The wind flip the grill 3 times in the yard, it look like a roll over car accident. The rubber wheels were on fire.

Fred heard the noise and woke up Uncle Bubba. Look across the street there's his neighbor from up the street Mr. August. Bubba hates his guts. He took about 100 pictures on his camera phone. Then jumped in his picked up and peeled off. Bubba was raging. Mr. August is basic and lies like a Political Program. He loves getting under Bubba's skin someone had already called the fire department.

After the grill flipped it looked like a F3 had hit it on one side. The 2 other sides had a butterfly effect. Spare ribs were dry crispy burnt. The corn was across the street in the neighbor's yard. The salmon wasn't recognizable. The crows immediately started eating it. The 6 baby back you could see them through the grill window. They looked fragile, and barely survived.

By now, the fire department gave him $200 fine. They can't figure out why he BBQ and sleep at the same time. Chief Brown said wait I have a grill just like that $700.00 it just came out. Is pops crazy? This is the 3rd time I've put a grill out. And it's always in May! Could this be historic? Sgt. Jason said, it looks hideous, like it was in the movie Fire Starter.

Meanwhile Bubba put's his grill on the wheelbarrow and rolled it to the backyard. The burnt/smoky aroma is all through the community. Some of the neighbors nodded and went inside. The buzzards, crows, and hawked flocked to the scene. They're having a feast.

Bubba glanced down the street and whistled for Fred to come home. He was talking to Mr. August. The same age as Bubba. Fred haste back to Bubba's what did that peeping Tom want? He said this is grill number six you done blew up. That you need 24 hours supervision, and fire department on stand-by before you cranked up another grill. Bubba has a red hot face.

He also stated you're the reason those crows are flying around. They are on stand-by waiting on the burnt ribs, they know where to find them. And lastly he has 4 of your burnt up grills on this camera phone. I've seen them with my own eyes.

Bubba's veins popping. "Whoa! This sucker talking about me like that? Go inside the house get my Remington – 12 gauge shotgun. And I got my G9 on my hip. I'm gonna go down there and empty a clip on that joker. Then Imma take his cell phone and delete all of his pictures. "That creep don't know me from a can of paint!"

Take it easy Bubba, he's got all these stray dogs running through here like pet cemetery. He keeps feeding them. "His lugnuts rattling in the hub caps." Let me prove it. Have you ever checked out his bumper sticker? Nah! It reads "Honk if you collect baby doll heads!" what an idiot. Fred had smoked him a joint and flipped over the grill and wheel barrow laughing. Fred said, something is wrong with both of you nuts.

Saturday Afternoon
Currently, Bubba's getting the baby backs outta the grill. Bubba had to get a crowbar to get them out. They were dry as the Mojave Desert. Imma fix this with some BBQ sauce. Hopefully Faye is turn up and won't notice. Wait! I got a question youll's burning up junk, then fixing it. Watcha talking about? Mama burned 3 cakes then she said she could fix them in 10 minutes. Hahaha! Faye must "been on some stuff!" She never burned anything up. Said Bubba.

Fred's getting curious in the backyard. I wonder what he been doing with all of them burn up grills? I know they ain't in the shed all of the tools are in there. I know he ain't been putting them on the back of his pick-up hauling them away. Nah! He wouldn't dare let his neighbors and Mr. August see that. I just gotta tip toe and search some more.

Food For Thought: Maybe he's paying the Moonshiner's to load and take them out to the woods at night. They like night movement. They just need a bit of magic, math, and science. It's just 21% alcohol and a few tweaks to their home made recipes. Fred's thinking about the race again, uhmm! I'm starting to lean towards Goldencents because he's a great horse. He can run on <u>dirt</u>, <u>grass</u>, and <u>Synthetic surfaces</u> etc. He has a quick burst of speed and favorable position. Plus he won the Santa Anita Derby, and I want Krigger to make history. Ughh! Too bad I don't have that $200.00

Thanks to Craig list. I didn't know they were Shady.

Chapter 5

Bubba said, Right away let's go! Fred ride shot-gun, we need to keep this little trouble on the down low. Then I won't tell Faye what happened to you, sometimes you act like a jive turkey. Let's shake on it. Where's the baked beans? They blew up with the grill. Somebody put the cast iron skillet on my porch. At least you still got a porch. Right on!

So Uncle Bubba which horse you rolling with Verrazana is my pick. Why? He has speed, love to run in the front of the pack. The wind is picking up again. I hope this rain slack up. The race is at 6pm. My horse is Golden Soul. Just like the Soul Brother James Brown. Crap! I can't make a bet thanks to Coco. Bubba said, Coco done already took you for a ride. You should never want to see any more horses. Hahaha! Uncle Bubba said, Golden Soul isn't a closer. He finished 4th in Louisiana Derby and he won't have any kick. Ughh!

The rain and wind is really coming down. Suddenly it's a thumping sound and a flat tire. We got 45 minutes left. Bubba said get out the truck. You're gonna learn how to fix a flat tire. In the rain? Yep! Fred kicked the rim and hurt his toe. Man I hate getting wet. What if I run up on me a honey! Bubba said, "You can't bust a grape!" Hahaha!

Saturday Evening an hour before the race
Hereafter Mama has everything in place. Still raining heavy, Shorty is standing in for Fred, Greeting guests and passing out horse pick-cards. Everything is set to start on time for the race. Everyone's having a good time. The ladies enjoyed the shopping spree. Cooked their signature food, played card games, horse shoes etc. The ladies have on some beautiful hats. The men and women wore their T-shirts Friday. Most of the men stuck with the sun hats and horse shoe mustaches. Betty can't wait to see Bubba so she can bat her eyes. Rico won the rose Trophy Cup.

Therefore, Mama has called Bubba again. Where you'll at? We had a flat, will be there shortly. OK! Bubba and Fred just walked in the door. Everyone is in TV room waiting on the race. A weather alert just came across the TV screen. A tornado warning is headed for all 3 countries including Madison. The party had to shut down. Everyone went to the storm shelter built in the basement. 50 people can be there.

Everyone took their drinks. And still having fun, socializing, telling stories. Mama was crushed tho, she put so much of work into this party. And now this? What else could happen.

Simultaneously, at Church Hills Down, the festivities are still going on. The horses been talking junk to each other all week. They want this race to be sloppy and quick. They're sick of crowd noises, rain, and loud music. The horses hate hearing My Old Kentucky Home song! The horses feel like it's too long. Check out the horse talk on the next page. Everyone received a copy upon entering the party. Oxbow said, "There's no more vibe in the atmosphere. I wanna hear the rapper Lil Baby!" Now they can blast that all over Kentucky.

Horse Drama at Churchill Downs:

You can't have a Derby Party without some Horse Animation. They bring excitement, enthusiasm and high energy. They know each other well, a whole week of training, vibrancy, vitality and liveliness.

They all have one thing in common. SuperEgos!

Fla. Derby Winner
Gate 16 – Morning line favorite
(7-2 Fav)
I bring versatility

Orb = I already have Derby success, flawless. I have late speed in the stretch and final furlogs. Yeah! You Shannagans already hatin on me because of post 1, the death post. Im'ma remain alive and vibrant. The sloppy track don't scare me, I'm a chaser. Yo! With Joel Rosario riding me I answer who want some? Normdy Invasion got beef with me. "When your Jocky Chad Brown win a Kentucky Derby Race come see me dog!"

Gate 3
10-1
<u>Revolutionary</u> = Winner of 3 straight races including the Louisiana Derby. I'm like a rapidity of speed and action. "You'll need to check my pedigree cuzz!" I'm a firecracker, Cuban missile. Who want some? I'm strong and solid blazing speed. Needs to avoid traffic as he make his push to front of pack. Revolutionary said, Golden Soul you wasn't even close to beating me in Louisiana Derby.

You ran out of gas in the stretch hommie.

Gate 5
3-1
<u>Normdy Invasion</u> = Yo! I'm a hard closer and late running. My last race I rode closer to the pace (wood Memorial) because of the slow place. I made up good ground on them fools. Verrazano wasn't the best horse on the field I was. That was a bunch of hog wash. Imma come with a surprise victory while you'll sleep. My running style gonna help me get the distance of the derby. He's got to go through and around a lot of horses if he's gonna work his way to the front in the stretch drive. My Lute said! That's where you will fade. And I will make my break to the stretch. Not worried dogg!

Gate 8
5-1
<u>Goldencents</u> = Ghee! Glad I got some training on the wet track. This will be a sloppy mess. You'll need to stop barking. I'm a serious contender, keep the negative opinions. I'm a grinder, don't need to be hard charging closer. Plus, Imma make history... My Jockey Kevin Kigger would be the first African American to win a Kentucky Derby. You'll feel me? Orb replied, I don't feel nothing but the rain. All week been listening to my song. Lil Nas X-Old Town Road - Ft. Billy Ray Cyrus. You'll know Bruh! "This will play in my head while I'm on the track. Who wanna pull up?"

Gate10
20-1
<u>Palace Malice</u> = Tired of the "drip drop rain." Yes, I finished in the Keenland Polytrackin Bluegrass. Java's War said Shut up! You choaked in traffic in two races. What's wrong with you? But this will be my 3rd race in 5 weeks. You cry too much, talking about I was stalking you.

Mike Smith is your jockey, I hope he whip you all the way to the finish line. Ughhh! "He don't use a whip on me cuzz." Whaterver!

Gate 14
4-1
<u>Verrazano</u> = Yep! I'm a favorite too. Sick of hearing about Orb. Check my record undefeated in 4 career starts. My tactical speed will keep me close to the leaders. Yo! I got high cruising speed over a distance of ground. I got plenty of gas in the tank Bruhhh! Normandy Invasion stay in your lane dogg! "You don't want this smoke!"

Horse Drama Cont:

<u>Mylute</u> is still hot with Revolutionary. The race should've been a tie. I was sprinting the whole race it was a stretch battle. I lost by a neck in the Louisiana Derby. He was running Gangsta Style all on my back.

Golden Soul said, you were on the rail at the top of the stretch with the pace makers, Then you choked when it was time for you to lead. "You shot Your Own Foot!"

Mylute told Golden Soul, shut up! I'd love to put a dent in your rear.

Golden Soul said, Nah! You don't wanna pull up on this smoke Bruh! I got some Perkiness I wanna show these whimps.

He told Mylute, you need to worry about Revolutionary.

He will be all up in your grill at the stretch.

Mylute replied, Seriously Punk! Bye Fool! You're already fading I can hear it in your voice. See you in the Far Turn. Haha!

Next: The race is finished and this is how it went.

Results of The Race:

1st place	Orb	5th	Mylute
2nd place	Golden Soul	6th	Oxbow
3rd place	Revolutionary	7th	Helene Super Star
4th place	Normandy Invasion	8th	Will Take Charge

Orb said, Yo! Where you'll at? I can't hear from nobody. Man this is a good feeling. Having the Run For The Roses" draped over me, for the whole world to see.

Orb railed from an early deficit for a thrilling Victory to the finish line. He had 2 ½ lengths followed by Golden Soul and Revolutionary to round out the top 3.

Orb was the favorite at 5-1 before the start Jockey Joel Rosario brilliantly navigated orb on an arduous, sloppy track. Orb was as far back as 15th before Rosario gave him the Jolt needed for a trip to the winner's circle. Orb is the fifth Champion to emerge from the No. 16 post position, which is the most successful starting point.

Epilogue

Uncle Bubba went to comfort her. Sis, you did a good job on this party. This storm gonna blow over and we gonna get this party started. Fred recorded the race. Oh! I wasn't even thinking about that. OK! So get these guest ready because we gonna get these card tables, pool tables, and chest tables going. Some are watching the pre-recorded race. Hollering and screaming. Imma throw on me so Bobby Womack and we gona get busy. I gotta get them baby backs out the car. Fred said, these people already drunk. Shorty said, they been drinking since 2pm. I got me a few sips of Peaches Moonshine. She left her purse in the bathroom. Man was my throat on fire. Fred said, Yo! Do the Amish priest need a shot. Nah! He been blowing up my phone Bruh! Shorty said, He don't want nothing! He just want to Beat A Dead Horse!

Mama's gonna continue to work on her long term goal and maybe start therapy again. -Fred was dealt with by mama. He had to wait longer before mama fixed his car. She took his car keys. He never got his phone back nor did he see Coco again. Him and Belinda is still working it out. Uncle Bubba and Mr. August are still fighting, Fred still continues his investigation on Bubba's missing grills. Shorty's still keeping his weight down for Jockey school.

Fred took China Sight Seeing. The ladies are getting ready to do one more shop till you drop! Shopping spree's tomorrow. Everyone will be leaving Monday and Tuesday returning home. Fred can't wait to get his room back for some chill time. He's gonna create a YouTube Video to Highlight and Showcase mama's Parties. He hopes to collaborate with Tyler Perry.

Finally, Uncle Bubba didn't get a chance to try out his Pineapple BBQ Sauce. The Priest didn't get a chance to call the cops. The storm came quick. Mama managed to get a call from a land Developer in Texas. Fred refused to give Shorty more information about the club. Fred stated I've never seen Uncle Bubba's passionate side. He calmed mama down quickly. Gotta give him a 5 star for that love he showed. Mylute nor Goldencents made history.

Second Series
Run For The Roses
41ST Kentucky Derby
Saturday May 2015
Churchill Downs

The whole world will be watching this Kentucky Derby Race, If American Pharoah win he will be the history's 12th Triple Crown Winner, "The Grand Slam".

This race could become Historic, by ending a 37-year Triple Crown drought.

American Pharoah and Dortmund are the 2 favorites:

Jockey:	**Jockey:**
Victor Espinoza	Martin Garcia
Trainer:	**Trainer:**
Bob Baffert	Bob Baffert

Everytime you turned on the Television, Radio, or Cellphone on they would hear about American Pharoah.

Another Sports Mom Party
2nd – Series

Introduction

Faye Wilson - Mama Faye is our Sports mom. This is her 2nd year hosting the Sports Mom Party. It's Therapy for her while working on a Reality Show. Everyone loves the perfumes that she wears and the beautiful rose bushes lined up in front of the house These Ladies know each other very well. They went to high school together, and have worked together on jobs, and putting on events in the past. It takes a year to plan for the Kentucky Derby Party. We are just a bunch of seniors having fun.

The Derby is always the first Saturday in May, rain or shine. We choose our horses but no gambling. The ladies start arriving on the Thursday before the big race. Frederick is there to assist with luggage and help the ladies get comfortable when they arrive. On Friday, we prepare foods for Saturday's event. Everyone brings or makes two food items and we have a round table talk about our hats. This year our color is white. Everyone wants Mama's Knock Down Potato Salad Recipe. She will be making quick luncheon rolls and banana split pie for this year's event.

Mama Faye is ready for the ladies to come visit. She has everything all cleaned up. She went out in her yard and cut some of the roses to make a beautiful center piece since everyone love to smell roses.

Betty Harris just turned 75 years old three days ago. She has the shortest drive. She lives in Macon, Georgia. It will take her about two hours to get to Athens, Georgia. She packed all of her Blue's CD's, and drives very well using her GPS. She sometimes gets lost with the GPS because she has no sense of direction.

She has brown bubbly eyes, and will bat them at Uncle Bubba, Also a Georgia Bulldog Fan. She loves spicy food but it gets her acid reflux inflamed. She has her own home remedies product from Jamaica to treat it. She loves the Jamaican hot wings. She made some last year and everyone's throats were on fire. She loves to party and play those down home blues. She is making Fried Georgia okra and Creeping Crust Cobbler.

<u>Aunt Peaches</u> is 69 years old. She will be leaving her home in Clanton, Alabama Thursday morning and making the four - hour drive to Athens, Georgia in three - hours by driving 90 mph in a 70 mph zone. She got pulled over last year but the cop thought she was Tina Turner. He asked for her autograph and told her to slow down before she killed someone. She put in her Tina Turner CD and kept rolling in her 5.0 Red Mustang Drop Top. She's riding with the top up so she doesn't mess her hair up. She is retired from the Post Office. She is very tight with money. She always carries extra pair of Daisy Dukes and White Lightning in her suitcase. Somehow the punch always gets spiked. Hmm. She is the life of the party. She will be making Aunt Karen's Drunken Chicken and Cole Slaw with a twist.

<u>Marlene Black</u> is 72 years old. She will be leaving on Wednesday afternoon and driving six hours from her home in Biloxi, Mississippi to Athens, Georgia. She is always prepared on her road trips. She likes taking her time and bringing her special pillow and blanket. Her cut off is three hours then it's time to get a room and get back on the road the next day.

She has gorgeous long hair that goes down her back. She can be shy and quiet at times. Her husband passed in 1990. She spends her time at the casinos and on EBay. She will be making fresh out of the Gulf of Mississippi fried catfish and her specialty drink, Mint Julep.

<u>Janetta Joseph</u> is 73 years old and will be coming from her home in Battle Creek, Michigan to Athens, Georgia which is a twelve - hour drive. She loves all the beautifully scented flowers of the south. Her daughter, China, will be driving her for six - hours; and her sweet, playful, spoiled, chocolate cocker spaniel, Roxy, will be coming along as well. She hates being alone. China will be babysitting Roxy when they arrive in Athens, Georgia. She will be making her New England Throw Down Shepherd's Pie and Honey Bourbon Glazed Ham. What a treat for everyone.

Fred said, "I don't know if we will ever hear from Uncle Eugene again. "It's been about 3 years since we last heard from him. I'm glad Yussef didn't turn out like Uncle Eugene a Hoodlum. Bubba said, I'm surprised they didn't jail him for espionage. Mama said, "You'll should've seen Bubba at the Smith Family Reunion.

He jacked up the ribs, it reminded me of the movie "Little Shops of Horrors." Bubba Said, Wait Faye you getting it mixed up. That was Ray-Ray. She Said, Ohhhh! They all laughed so hard. Bubba stated now that dude is dangerous on a grill, please don't let him Start the fire And Imma stop right there because you never know he might show up at one of these parties. His first question will always be, "Who Cooked The Ribs? Like he's the king of BBQ! He's the half Brother from a different mother. Him and Bubba is 8 months apart.

Chapter 1

Uncle Bubba is Faye's brother who grills all of the meats and brings them over on Saturday. We like to call him "rib burner" because he's always getting distracted and burning the meat. On Friday night, we have a round table meeting to discuss our horses and play cards and dominos. Nobody can slam the bones on the table like Aunt Peaches. She's a radical! Frederick likes to eaves drop on the seniors conversations. They are hilarious. He gets on Mama's nerves when he has on his headphones blasting that rap music. His favorite foods are the fried fish and potato salad and he will tear up that creeping cobbler. It is amazing.

He loves the old fashioned country cooking that these ladies do. If a man doesn't work, you best believe he isn't eating any food so I've been working hard helping them out because I got to eat. My best friend SYLVESTER is Amish. He wants to try some of our soul food. I told him, "line bait and sinker, you will be hooked once you try it". Mama said she will make sure he gets a plate. Sylvester-AKA (Shorty), Frederick = AKA (Fred)

It's midday on Thursday and everyone is arriving at different times. Fred is helping everyone to get settled in their rooms. He began to wonder why these ladies' suitcases are so heavy. Some of them packed like they are running away from home. I don't get it. Aunt Peaches' luggage is the heaviest. I thought about getting a pallet jack to move the luggage to the front door. I don't know how I'm going to get it upstairs, and to top it off she has six Alabama watermelons in her trunk. We have enough of their stuff here to do a Farmer's Market. I didn't see all of this coming! Shorty said, "Where's the corn? Probably where she keeps her moonshine. Underneath the spare tire. Shorty looked bewildered! Shorty wanted Fred to explain that later. We became good friends when he moved in next door last year. We have a lot in common. I had to beg his parents to let him do his senior year in the public school. He was tired of being homeschooled because farming overruled his home schooling. He is ready to be an independent young man, not a farmer for life. His parents are not so friendly.

<u>Well, It's Thursday evening</u> and everyone has settled in and has eaten dinner. We are gathering around the round table for the Hat Talk. This is where we share something about our hats and style. The host of the party always chooses the color of the hats for that year. Mama Faye chose White!

Some of the women usually prepare their foods ahead. Too save time well white hats for this year. Janetta Joseph will be our host for next year in Battle Creek, Michigan.

Aunt Peaches boyfriend, Raymond surprised her with this beautiful cream color hat with a black ribbon around it and white polka dots all over the ribbon. He paid $ 106 for that hat at the Mall of America. In Minnesota, He's a Successful Businessmen who loves Southern women. Bubba, Said, He's Gatta be Super Slow!

Marlene Black went on EBay and purchased her white feathered hat for $ 35. The original price was $ 89. I love chasing sales.

Janetta Joseph found her beautiful cream hat with stripes around the rim for $20 at a yard sale. The original price was $66. She had to wheel and deal for the lower price.

Betty Harris purchased her hat three weeks after the 2014 Kentucky Derby at JC Penny for $40. It's all white with beautiful yellow lace around the brim and white feathers in the back. The original cost was $150. She like to wear it to church and funerals.

Mama Faye picked her hat up at the last minute. She had run up on a sale at Sears. The hats were marked down 30% off. Her hat was white with pink buttons around it. She paid $36 for it.

Uncle Bubba orders pizza and wings for everyone for the night. Tomorrow's going to be a long day for everyone. Betty Harris will be getting up and making breakfast for everyone. Then each of the ladies will start preparing their dishes for Saturday's Derby. It's called the busy kitchen. Everyone laughed.

Horse Talk At The Table

Everyone just got finished eating breakfast. Marlene just can't get over how good those Kentucky grits were. She wants her secret recipe. We listed a few of the contenders below. Some of these names come from: Horse Date Bases, owners, breeders and families.

# 18 American Pharaoh	# 9 Bolo
# 10 Firing Line	# 17 Mr. Z
# 8 Dortmud	# 1 Ocho Ocho Ocho
# 5 Danzig Moon	# 20 Far Righr
# 3 Materiality	# 19 Up Start
# 13 It's A Knockout	# 15 Frosted
# 2 Carpe Diem	# 14 Keen Ice

Some of these horses are not stranger to each other. Some have raced in the same races below before making it to the Kentucky Derby.

- Preakness Stakes
- Belmont Stakes
- Santa Anita
- Arkansas Derby
- Blue Grass Stakes
- Breeders Cup
- Florida Derby
- Wood Memorial Stakes
- Ohio Derby
- Smarty Jones Stakes

My Horse Selections

It's Friday evening and all of the food is prepped for Saturday afternoon. Now we will have another round table to discuss which horses we choose.

Uncle Bubba-firing Lane

Mama Faye: American Pharoah

Betty Harris: Firing Lane

Aunt Peaches: Materiality

Marlene Black: Far Right

Janetta Joseph: Frosted

Fred: It's A Knockout

Fred: This is my secret horse. I'm betting online just like my Uncle Bubba. Do they think I'm going to be the butler around here and not bet on a horse? I'm going to bet $150 online on my horse I started saving for this last year and besides I'm learning from the best, my Uncle Bubba.

Fred just got finished talking to Uncle Bubba. He is supposed to be preparing the ribs and meats for tomorrow. Bubba will cook them at 1:00 PM on Saturday and he will drop them off before 5:00 PM. He said that gives him plenty of time to cook them. My ribs will fall off the bone. That's scary Uncle Bubba. I had to turn my head and sneak a laugh to myself, knowing them ribs will be burnt to the bone. I don't know why we let him cook those ribs knowing that he always burns them. They sure aren't cheap. Fred is still puzzled about all of the hype for a 2-minute horse race. I just know this horse is missing his tail, and I don't even want to hear about the back story.

Now, American Pharaoh is expected to win the Kentucky Derby and The Triple Crown Race. He is supposed to be the fastest horse on the track. Before these seniors can bat an eye the race will be over.

These women are so turned up and don't know how to turn down. I got me a new cell phone, top of the line. I'm getting ready to turn-up my contenders list. # 13 It's A Knockout will be my horse. The odds of him winning are 30-1. I like the name because all of the ladies will be knocked out by 5:00 PM the day of the race. I found out that these races are for the rich and famous, not the blue collar workers. "Save every penny. "Hahaha! Because, ain't no Kentucky Derby Party like mama's

Mama said, take great pleasure in having your own Kentucky Derby Party. It's all about bringing people together having a good time like back in the day. Once the race is finished, it's party time with mixed drinks and mint julep for the whole state of Kentucky. Even the horses' party, especially the Winner with roses draped over his back.

Frederick said he is already burnt out trying to keep these seniors comfortable. I need somebody to make me comfortable. I should be chasing girls right now. I'm a young blood. Mama Faye went into the family room and put on some blues. B. B. King, Muddy Waters, and Bobby Blue Band. I told Mama this is supposed to be a Kentucky Derby Party. Aunt Peaches said, it's a Sports Mom Party, with a loud voice and we don't need children hanging around. Fred looked surprised. What! I'm 17 years old and grown. I got cousins under me, and this horse channel is driving me crazy. Over and over I think all of them have a touch of O.C.D., Obsessive Compulsive Disorder, because they won't let me change the channel. Every time I go into my room to chill they are calling me. I'm not the butler. Mama needs a nanny. Now, 1 do like the fact that China came along. She is supposed to be video tapping and dog sitting. She has her hands full and I need to be at Uncle Bubba's house at 1:00 PM on Saturday to help bring the meats here. These ladies are really having a good time and working me like a slave. Mama Faye cooked breakfast. We are eating good.

It's Saturday, Fred just called Uncle Bubba and no answer, this sounds like trouble. I know he has abused the ribs. I'm one mile away from his house at the 4 way stop and what do I smell and see? Ribs burning and smoke signals. Only if these ladies knew-the back story of Mr. Rib Burner. He's always got to clean up before he goes around them like he's some deacon.

I just arrived at the house and smoke is everywhere. The Fire Department just left, the coals are still red hot, so I ran in the house and put on the hotdogs, hamburgers, and smoke sausage. I woke up Uncle Bubba and ask him, where are the ribs? I thought you cooked 6 slabs? I did and they all burnt to the bone. I had just went inside and took a 30-minute nap and I believe those boys across the street was messing with my grill. I was breaking in my new grill. Before I took my nap, I went online to BetAmerica.com to place my bet on Firing Lane. Fred said, "You be tweaking" (nonsense). At least they have some type of grill meats." Glad I ain't in your shoes, said Fred. Bubba said, Right on!

Fred said help me to place my bet on "It's a Knock Out". He said, OK, since you're showing signs of becoming a man! We have to hurry up and drop this meat off what are you going to tell Mama Faye? I don't know. I'll think of something on the way. I wanted to invite China over but she has to video and dog sit at the party. He said "Ok. We will talk about it on the way." Bubba said, she's a little too old for you. Maybe but I got the juice, said Fred. They both laughed so hard.

Fred looked at Uncle Bubba's $800 grill and said "this is no way to break in a new grill. Can you just give up your grill license?" What! Uncle Bubba snapped. Do you know how long it took me to get these license? I had three grilling crash courses and maxed out on all three. After that course they told me I was a barbequing professional. Do you get a rush off burning ribs to the bone? Boy! You need to hush your mouth! I'm not bothering anyone. I didn't catch anything on fire. Captain Woods from the fire department is one of my good friends. We go way back into the day. At one time in our life we were O.G.'s (old gangsters). Frederick said, I can't even imagine you being an O.G. Uncle Bubba said madly, "can you picture me busting a cap in your behind?' He said, Boy, don't you even try me! I keep telling you I'm a fool but I'm not an old fool! Now get into the truck so we can drop off these meats. We don't need to be late. But, uncle all of your grills look like they crashed. Uncle Bubba said, "Shut up wooden head!"

While on the way to Mama's house, Frederick had a lot of stuff on his mind. He began to think to himself, Uncle Bubba is crazy for real. Maybe he was an O.G. because he done snapped on me like a real gangster. Maybe he is nervous about being around all of those ladies. What is he running from? Imma keep searching for those burnt up grills. He has a collection hidden somewhere, like it's a hobby.

Back at Mama's house we are all set to take pictures for our scrap book. We got our hats on and horses picked out. If one of their horses win, they're going crazy up in here! It's still a party in here. Janetta just came from her car with a stack of blues cd's. She said blues, mix drinks, and playing card goes together. She is missing one other thing, her 26-year-old boyfriend! Aunt Peaches said, I thought you had back problems. She said, Girl, I got pain killers for that problem, talk to the hand. They continued their card game.

China is still filming but decided to put Roxy down stairs in the basement. She is very irritating and almost got stepped on twice. Everything is too loud for her. China was scared to taste that Mint Julep, because these women are boarder line alcoholics.

Mama went into the kitchen to check on the Drunken Chicken and cut up the ribs. She is looking everywhere for those ribs. They are not on the stove. She called Bubba and Fred into the kitchen. She wanted to know what happened to the ribs. Ughhh! Looking at each other.

As evidenced, Fred got a little closer to Bubba. He really wanted to hear his answers. Especially since he was an O.G. Faye said please don't tell me you burned up all 6 slabs of ribs with your brand new $800 grill which is half gas, half charcoal! Could you have put 3 in the smoker? I didn't have any hickory wood for the smoker and I got side tracked and went into the house for a quick nap. Mama was teed off greeting her teeth. She said, how many grill fries have you had? He said, none of your business. Mama stated you fool! But Tanner came through as a back up.

Rib burner, I'm giving you once more chance. You either get it together or leave it alone because I've been holding my breath for a long time. All of your money is spent on ribs and grills. You might want to take some grill classes this fall before someone snap your picture and post it on Crime Stoppers! Fred was bent over laughing, Bubba just stood there crazy looking smoking that stankin pipe!

Hey! Ease up on me sis! I will have it for next year's Sport Mom Party! They fired me from the Family Reunion Master Grill. I can't afford for you to fire me too. I think my medication may be the cause of me falling asleep. I've been taking it at 7:00 AM just as prescribed. Right on!

Afterward, Fred said that don't sound right. Maybe it says to take it at 7:00 PM. No Dude! I've been taking it like this for a long time and everything felt normal. Fred said sure! And let it go. Uncle Bubba needed to use the bathroom. He was in a rush and ran into Betty. Boy was she turned up. She had a big smile for him and winked her left eye at him three times. Then she slipped him her number. He melted away and told Fred to start the truck. He needed to hurry up before he get himself into some trouble. I usually don't have anyone trying to hit on me. Back in the day I was rolling stone. But, I would like to hit it and quit it. Hahaha! Fred thought to himself this dude couldn't hit a Tee Ball.

Fred was supposed to be in the truck but he was checking out China. She is 19-years-old, very bright, 6'3 with a beautiful brown complexion with long blonde hair. She is built like a brick house. She graduated High School in 11th Grade. She wants to attend College in South West. She wants to be a Freelance Photographer. I told her I would get with her later. She and Fred have some things in common. He hates taking care of Dixie.

On the way to Bubba's house he told Fred. "You know I still like to look. I guess I have gotten too wrapped up with fishing, grilling and becoming a Mater Grill." I seen Ms. Betty I got her number. Why don't you use it? Maybe she is lonely too. I'll have to think about it. Everyone is talking.

Fred said, Uncle everyone know you're a Master Griller. What's so hard about giving up your grill license? I wonder if a girlfriend would help you get off that grill. You're becoming more and more dangerous. Plus you already spent about $8,000 on new grills." Bubba said, Fool why you all in my bank account? I'm spending all of my money before I kick the bucket."

Bubba said, It's three things Imma have in life. My grills, grill license and women. Plus, "I don't suffer from insanity – I enjoy every minute of it. " Right on! "Can you feel ME?" Fred looked like a blank sheet of paper. Mama said, "Fred why is your cat always screaming and crying?" Huh! Are you abusing Dixie? Nah! She's just spoiled. Mama said, don't make me call animal cruelty on you. But, she keeps hiding and tearing up my new Jordans. Uncle Bubba said, so what! Pumping on his cigar. Now the whole house smell like a barn. Bubba told Fred, a dog has an owner, a cat has a staff. Leave Dixie alone creep. Fred shrugged his shoulders!

Bubba stated, By the way Faye. When I'm doing the ribs, I don't need no back up. Tanner is just another mis-Fit in the community. No one told him to put a whole hog on the grill. He's always tryna Show Out. Mama said, I knew you would fly The Coop and Show up empty handed. Just like today. What's your point Faye?

To tell the truth, I'm the only grill King here in Athens. Mama said, that's when you was younger. Bubba you just don't have it anymore.

You blew up, burned up, 40 grills in the last 3 years. That's not normal. Bubba's Steaming! Faye. It's not normal for you too still be making moon shine either. Mama turned a blind eye to his comment and left. Seriously!

Chapter 2

Next, about those Kentucky Grits Mama Faye Made. Food is all on the table. Everyone is ready to throw down. Mama just remembered to make a plate for Shorty. He has never eaten Soul food.

Meanwhile, Roxy is downstairs having a hissy fit because she doesn't like being alone. She has gotten into Fred's closet and is pulling down clothes, chewing on his shoes, football, and a love letter that was on his closet floor. Dixie is Fred's cat. She is scared of Roxy. Dixie has climbed on top of the dresser. Roxy is barking like crazy. She finally got tired and fell asleep on the pile of clothes in the closet.

China keeps trying to make it downstairs to Roxy but keeps getting distracted. She looks worn out. Roxy is spoiled and high maintenance. Mama treats Roxy like she is a baby. She sometimes likes to snap on China when she is over stimulated. China will hold back on her doggie treats and make her calm down.

Fred tells China this party is off the chain because they didn't need any mix drinks because you can get drunk off the food. What do you mean Fred? It's this white corn liquor. Known as white lightening. Homemade liquor from back in the day. How do you know so much about this liquor young blood? Well, my Uncle Bubba told me all about it. He used to have a whisky still. Ok. Guess I will try the New England's Shepard's Pie. She thought the Shepard's Pie was okay to eat. Fifteen minutes later, her head was spinning like a hot dryer. She was about to go check on Roxy but now she has to sober up first. The loud music only made her problem worse.

Somehow Roxy is out and upstairs. Janetta was getting her groove on. Her favorite song was playing "Shot Gun" from back in the day. Aunt Peaches had five plastic BB guns in the trunk of her car. She ran out to get them. All of the ladies got one. They simulated shooting each other through the whole song. Mama Faye was laughing so hard tears were coming out of her eyes.

As evidenced, Peaches threw her wig off two hours ago and Roxy found it. She is chewing away and no one is paying attention. Everyone is turned up and feeling good and that includes China. The race will be starting soon. Mama Faye is having a hard time trying to get them back on the track. This is the hardest things she has ever done. She is glad someone else will be hosting the party next year. These parties are not feeling like therapy anymore. I am being over worked and it usually takes me a week to get back on track.

Fred said, Peaches need to keep that wig on. That ball spot looks a mess. Who perm and dye their hair on the same day. She's lucky it was just a ball spot.

Mama stated, I'm taking me a serious vacation after this party. Fred is going to stay with my brother until I return. Fred said, under his breath. Not happening! Bubba's a complete fool. The Derby race will be starting in twenty minutes and Roxy has the best seat in the house (recliner).

Aunt Peaches just put on Mustang Sally. It's an oldie but a good one. Everyone got up and started dancing. This is Betty's favorite and she is ready to throw down so she cranked up the volume. China is holding her head up while tripping on a dog toy. Shucks!

She finally asked Mama Faye for an Advil PM and if someone else could finish the recording. Mama Faye is still trying to get everyone quiet and calmed down. The race is beginning to start. The women just kept right on partying so Mama Faye joined in. Mr. August never showed up. Faye's classmate Fred's been looking for him all night. So we missed out on the Kentucky Fried Chicken. The most important food item. Fred knew the energy at the party would shift. He's probably somewhere turning up his Pickle Jar of Moonshine. Also Mama is about to loose it, She's tired of hearing Mr. August raggedy, run-down, ratty truck. He's been up and down the street 6 times today. Some fool put a catback exhaust on it. He wanted a diesel roar sound, where's the dignified Priest now? Fred stated, the loud noise give Mr. August a rush!

The Race will start in two minutes and Roxy is in the recliner enjoying the horse race and wagging her tail until the race was finished. Another two-minute race has come and gone. The ladies are back at the table playing cards and dominoes.

RUN FOR THE ROSES

141st KENTUCKY DERBY – MAY 1.25 MILES

IT'S TIME FOR HORSE TALK:

These contenders are in their post position.

Some of us don't like the sloppy track due to the rain earlier.

The horses usually have a few minutes before the race starts. If they could really talk to each other their conversations may go a little like this:

Position:	Name:	Odds:
#1	Ocho Ocho Ocho	50-1
	I'm in a tough spot but I'm not crying. My name is Spanish for the word eight In case fans wanted to talk about me! By the way, I ride in style with my good balance so don't play me close.	
#2	Carpe Diem	8-1
	I love the middle post. I want to make it known I'm usually the favorite. I respect American Pharaoh for this race I really want to rob him of his Triple Crown Dreams.	
#3	Materiality	12-1
	I'm in a good gate to get out quickly. Yeah! I heard you all talking about my throat Surgery, but has nothing to do with my strong pedigree. I'm a serious player. Check me out in the Florida Derby.	
#4	Tencendur	30-1
	I'm speechless don't have time for these Drama Kings.	
#5	Danzig Moon	30-1
	I like being in the back of the pack so I can just roll up on everyone at the right moment.	
#6	Mubtaahij	20-1
	I'm the only one breed from the Ireland. I don't wear my horse shoes when training. I have great speed.	

| #7 | <u>El Kabeir</u> | 30-1 |

They scratched me from the Kentucky Derby. I'm upset with my left foot issues. My speed is consistently fast.

| #8 | <u>Dortmund</u> | 3-1 |

Yeah! I'm big and strong even though I lost my horse shoe in a race this year. I dreamed about having post 20. I like dirt and being on the outside. My quickness will keep me in the mix.

| #9 | <u>Rolo-Twin</u> | 30-1 |

<u>Kolo</u> is my twin and we both won the Eddie Logan Stakes at Santa Anita as two year olds. Sometimes they can't tell us apart but I will be rolling in this race like the Alabama Crimson Tide! Roll Tide!

| #10 | <u>Firing Line</u> | 12-1 |

Yeah! I heard everyone talking about the old man, Gary Stevens, my Jockey. He's won three Kentucky Derby's. I've lost two races to Dortmund. My sore right foot is fixed and I'm ready to get it on. Whip me to the finishing line.

| #11 | <u>Stanford</u> | 30-1 |

Straight up the middle is how I will run, but I just found out that they scratched me off for Frammento.

| #12 | <u>International Star</u> | 20-1 |

Won the Louisiana Derby. I won't think about my injury in this race.

| #13 | <u>It's A Knock Out</u> | 30-1 |

I love my post straight up the middle. I'm a deader because I love to train. I usually win.

| #14 | <u>Knee Ice</u> | 30-1 |

I'm the perfect post. Just in case someone wanted to know. I'm all out here by myself being celebrity. I got some issues but won all three starts at Church Hill Downs. I have momentum and courage while thinking about Run For The Roses. My plan is to steal someone's thunder.

#15   <u>Fosted</u>   15-1
            I love the auxiliary gate. I have some room to break.
            Everyone loves my pretty gray coat in spite of my injured
            shun problem. I'm a straight shooter. I don't like to drift
            off. My style is close running and no one intimidates me.

#16   <u>War Story</u>   50-1
            Yeah! Everyone wants to hear my stories, but I'm in a
            successful post and not fearful of anyone and that's my
            story.

#17   <u>Mr. Z</u>   50-1
            I'm tired of finishing 2nd of 3rd in thirteen races. They all
            talk about my habits veering off in the stretch. I've got it
            together and I'm ready for the big race. I had four lengths
            on Far Right in the Smarty Jones Race. Far Right came
            out of no where in the stretch and right now I'm ready to
            get in on like Marvin Gay.

#18   <u>American Pharaoh</u>   22-1
            I have a lot to say even though I wear ear plugs when
            racing. I did manage to hear all the Drama being talked
            in the post position. I'm not worried about Mr. Z who bit
            my tail off. A short tail gives me more speed. Firing line
            and Dortmud all got creamed by me in the Arkansas Derby
            where I had an eight length win. I have the power to take
            it home, so check with my Jockey Victor Espinoza.

#19   <u>Up-Start</u>   15-1
            This is the exact position for me. I got beef with materiality.
            He robbed me the Florida Derby. I like to keep the pace
            early and surge late. I want to warn all of you. Don't go
            to sleep on me.

#20   <u>Far Right</u>   30-1
            I have a touch of white on my forehead. I'm easy to deal
            with in the stall. I was runner up in the Florida Derby.
            I love the dirt track. The post position won't affect my
            running style. These other horses are jealous of me because
            I love being pampered. Now, watch me sit in the cut and
            do my thing.

| #21 | Frammento | 50-1 |

First of all, I'm running this race for Stanford. Who got scratched. He never made it to the gate. My name is an Italian word for Splinter. I was bought out of a sale. My trainer sent me to a farm to relax and I ran into a fence. These contenders think I'm blind and they stay away from me, but never under estimate a splinter. Standford said, shut up Roughneck!

| #22 | Tale of Verve | 22-1 |

I came in 2nd Place at the Preakness. My health and fitness is good. Well, Rested My style is running late and losing them in stretch. 1.5 miles run is a piece of cake for me even on a wet track. I will still be running when the race is over. Me and the track star Usaine Bolt think alike. We both have speed.

American Pharaoh said, Tale of Verve "I ain't tryna hear none of this. You should be ready by now, plus your character flaws always show up. You're clumsy, always losing your horse shoe and falling over dirt on the track.

Tale of Verb said, Yo! Don't go there! You're spoiled and bratty, and self-centered. Tired of hearing your name across the Country, TV and Radio. Like you're some Hollywood Celebrity. Yeah! You got speed but you're too pre-occupied with your physical appearance. American Pharaoh said, Get Ready for the Race Looser.

Tale of Verb said, Wait! I ain't finished, I know your back story. You use to race with blinkers and cotton was put in your ears to ease your sensitivity to noise. So, "Sweep round your own front Door first." And your Jockey Victor Espinoza need to break out that whip on you.

American Pharaoh stated, I have bigger fish to fry. My Jockey don't need a whip with speed like mine. So get on the dirt track, you will fade before the far turn. Bye bye!

Dortmund said, wait Mr. Pharaoh we have same trainer. Imma be on you like a cheetah, I know all of your flaws, failings, and fears. I even know about your secret fracture. American Pharaoh said "BOY BYE!"

RUN FOR THE ROSES

141st KENTUCKY DERBY – MAY 2015

<u>IT'S TIME TO GET IT ON!</u> The race we been waiting for:

And they're off: American Pharaoh broke ok. Firing Line in the early mix. Carpe Diem is there. Dortmund sets the pace. It's a knock out. Frosted and War Story make their way to the back stretch. Dortmund is leading by 0.5 length. Firing Line in 2nd, Carpe Diem follows in 4th place, Mr. Z., Ocho Ocho Ocho, here comes the American Pharaoh AND THEY'RE IN THE STRETCH! American Pharaoh on the outside and takes the lead. Firing Line is not done yet. They are neck and neck. American Pharaoh, the favorite takes the race. He wore everyone down. Fire Line, 2nd place. The horse without a tail showed up again. He can't wait to be draped in those beautiful red roses for all the world to see.

The pace were solid up front with <u>Dortmund</u> and <u>Firing Line.</u> After ½ mile in 47.34, and 3 length gap separating the leader Dortmund and the 4th place winner (Carpe Diem) By the ¾ mile mark the gap between the lead group of Dortmund, Fire Line, and American Pharaoh stayed static at about 3 lengths, but American Pharaoh began to close in on the leader. American Pharaoh kicked 5 wide coming into the stretch, his speed kicked in.

At the 300-yard mark he pulled even with Dortmund and Firing Line. From there, he shifted to 3rd gear and it was over. He ran the perfect race and Victor Espinoza was just along for the ride. American Pharaoh will now move on to the 2nd leg of the Triple Crown Winner, the Preakness stake with a shot to make history as the first Triple Crown Winner since Affirmed back in 1978. Dortmund and Firing Line are both seeking a rematch in the Preakness.

<u>Derby Winners:</u>

(1.) American Pharaoh Jockey – Victor Espinoza
(2.) Firing Line – Jockey – Gary Stevens
(3.) Dortmund – Jockey - Martin Garcia
(4.) Frosted – Jockey – Joel Rosario
(5.) Danzig Moon – Julien Leparoux
(6.) Materiality – Javier Castellano

It was a two minute race! It just happened so quick. Mama Fay's doorbell is ringing like crazy. It woke up Roxy and she is at the door barking away. Mama Faye answered the door. It's the new neighbor who moved in next door last year. An Amish man with a white long beard and black suite. Mr. Father Ruben is my name. Mama Faye introduced herself and ask how could she help him. He asked her to turn down the music. They are trying to eat dinner and do bible study. She said, sure! Mama Faye went back into the house and turned the music down even though it's only 4:30 p.m.

Well mama thought she had settled that until she seen the five police cars rolling up in her yard as if it was some type of home invasion. Blue lights everywhere. The Street is lit up! The officer said, "Mama Faye, what kind of party is this?" My Annual Sports Mom Party. Mama Faye was curious and ask the officer who called the police? Mr. Father Ruben did. You know he don't care for English people. He reported that you have been out of control since Thursday afternoon and he hasn't been able to sleep or meditate.

So did Mr. Father Ruben tell you about the illegal farm animals he has there? I didn't complain when that poor Billy goat was running around in his yard screaming and begging for life! Every two months they have a goat roast on the grill. I don't know where all of these animals are coming from. He has all kinds of coon and possum traps and chicken feed in his yard. And to top it off, he is out there feeding crows. He even told his son, Shorty not to hang out with Fred anymore because he is a bad influence and too dark. Fred stated, without a doubt I got this mama!

Officer Bird stated, I can't wait to get off this shift. I think i'm going to eat that Drunken Chicken tomorrow because i'm wore out. I feel like those seniors knocked out at Mama Faye's house. I have never seen such active seniors. I did wonder about one thing though. Why didn't someone offer Mr. Father Ruben a plate to go! Are you kidding! Mr. Father Ruben is pure Godly man! According to his bible he has never sinned. Only the English people sin. Officer West said, "It seems like he has some serious, deep, dark, sketchy issues. Someone need to take him down to the creek to get dipped four or five times! He might just snap after he sees the results of Shorty's behavior after eating the Soul food. We might have to come back out and arrest someone.

It's 10:00 p.m. on Saturday night. Everyone is dog tired and drunk. Roxy is taking care of herself. China is crashed out on the couch. Mama Faye is cleaning up in the kitchen and fred just got home and he's asking mama Faye who won the Kentucky Derby. He said, "You all don't know! I thought this was the whole purpose to have the Derby Party!"

Well, they all got drunk off the mint Juleps, Drunken Chicken and Shepherd's pie. "Mama! The only thing straight was the Creeping Cobbler." How do you know that? "I sampled everything on the buffet. Now that Drunken Chicken and Shepherd's pie was on fire. Is there any of it left mama?" No boy, Officer Bird and his partner got the last two plates and I put away a plate for Shorty. "Why were the police here?" Our neighbor Mr. Father Ruben, called the police on us and he don't want his son, Shorty, hanging out with you anymore. He said, "Why? That's my best friend and he is getting ready to transition into the real world. He's tired of smelling like goat milk and farm animals every day. Shorty, made it real clear to me that he doesn't want to be a farmer. He wants to party and chase the girls too, like any normal teenager would be doing."

Sorry Mama. I got off track when you mentioned Mr. Father Ruben. Please answer my question Fred! Ok Mama. Are you ready for this? The winner of the Derby this year is American Pharaoh.

Mama scream so loud it woke up a few other ladies and they went back to sleep. Mama scared me. I didn't know she could get so loud. She asked, "Who came in the second place?" Firing Line. I did record the race because everyone was turned up except for Roxy. She said, "We will watch the race on Sunday after breakfast. All of the food is gone. No more drunks. I'm the hostess and needed to stay sober. I did eat the quick luncheon rolls, pizza and Creeping Cobbler. I drank 1/2 class of Mint Julep and it had some kind of kick like a mule. Even though I wanted to open up a can on Mr. Father Ruben. I wanted to grab my 9mm Smith & Wesson hand gun and deal with him, but decided to refrain. Dang!

To sum up, It's Sunday morning. Everyone is up and ready to eat breakfast except for Marlene. She has a terrible hangover and needs to sleep in a little longer. China is up. She went downstairs to check on Roxy. She couldn't find Roxy. She was breathing hard and out of breath. Fred told her to calm down. I will help you find Roxy. They went back to the house and run into Mama and said "Something is wrong! We can't find Roxy!" She is okay. She is out in the doghouse sleeping. She was up all night being overstimulated. Roxy was into everything downstairs. The place looks like a twister hit it. China looked surprised and said "Is it that bad?" He said, "Yes. Let's get working before Mama Faye comes down here and blows a gasket." Shorty said, "What does that mean? You all know I'm lost when it comes to using slang." That means Mama Faye is really mad. Steam starts to come out of her ears. She might use a few choice words and won't care who is around. Shorty is also helping them. When he got to the bottom steps he said, "This looks like a pig pen and it smells like one too. But don't worry. I'm used to cleaning them up." They all laughed and said Shorty is so funny. China asked Fred how he felt after eating the Drunken Chicken. He said, "I only got a baby food spoonful of everything before I went to my Uncle Bubba's house. The cobbler was so good I couldn't taste Drunken Chicken or the Shepherd's Pie. The cobbler overpowered it. Dang!

Undoubtedly everyone is rested up and ready to watch the pre-recorded Derby Race. As the race starts everyone is screaming and hollering for their horse to win. Roxy up again. She came into the house and watched the race for the second time. Firing line was up for the challenge while he hung in there with American Pharaoh, the favorite. He had to show everyone including American Pharaoh what speed he had. He went on and took 2nd place in case people wanted to test his speed. Aunt Peaches kept rewinding and rewinding about six times even though her horse, Materiality, was nowhere in the picture.Yikes!

Finally, everyone enjoyed the Sports Mom Party. Marlene said, "It was the best ever." Janetta, from Battle Creek Michigan will be our hostess for next year. Hopefully all of the snow will be gone by May. The ladies got to know each other better and formed relationships including Fred and China. He got a chance to take her sightseeing. They are getting ready to shop until they drop for the rest of the day.

Everyone will be leaving on Monday going back home and Fred can't wait to get back into his room to chill. He said these old Folks are slow and bossy. I still can't believe American Pharaoh's Speed on that track. He's gonna continue his grill investigation. Mamas still waiting for the big moment to hear from Tyler Perry.

A record crowd 170,513 was on hand to witness American Pharaoh's triumph. Race fans and horse lovers from around the world rejoiced American Pharaoh's success. Following his Triple Crown Achievement he returned to Churchill Downs where nearly 30,000 cheering fans watched owners Zayats stables, Trainer Bob Baffert, and Jockey Victor Espinoza - were awarded their Keepsake Kentucky Derby and Triple Crown Trophies. Capturing the heart of many American Pharaoh made it to the cover of Sports Illustrated and was pictured for the fashion, Beauty and celebrity Magazine, Vogue. -(Historic). Kentucky Native Ashley Judd Voiced the Opening for the telecast of the race, and was the first women to do so.

Victor Espinoza - Who is also the brother of Jose Espinoza (a Jockey also) A Mexican Jockey, 5 foot 2 in. He grew up on a farm Northwest of Mexico City. Worked as a bus driver while he took riding lessons and attended Jockey School. In 1993 he moved to Northern California, where he was leading apprentice Jockey. Moved to Los Angeles, Gained National attention in 2000 rode his first Kentucky Derby in 2001 came in 3rd. Espinoza's first Triple Crown was in 2002 aboard War Emblem. Then in 2015 he became the first Jockey with a consecutive shot at Triple Crown. American Pharaoh became the 12th Triple Crown winner and the first since Affirmed in 1978, and Espinoza, who was 43 was the oldest Jockey to capture the Triple Crown. He's won the Kentucky Derby 3 times, Triple Crown in 2015. He's been given the Prestigious George Wolf Memorial awarded by a vote of his peers. He's won 12 Southern California meet riding titles and He was inducted into the Sports Hall of Fame in 2017. All of that took a Back Seat when his 90-year old mother fractured her back while at home in Mexico. Mom needed her son's help. (younger son) Jose Espinoza was there. Victor took some time off for family. She was in the hospital for 3 weeks and he was right there by her side. She underwent therapy and is now back at home. His sister is helping too.

On July 28, 2018 Victor suffered a severe neck injury during a frightening training accident at Del Mar that left some wondering if he'd ride again. He was 46 yrs. Old and was riding Bobby Abu Dhabi during a training run. When suddenly the horse had a heart attack and collapsed with Victor on top.

He suffered a fractured vertebrae as well as injuries to his neck and left arm. At first he was worried because he couldn't feel his arms and legs. But the feeling came back. His doctors said, he will need time and patience as he recovers and continuous his rehabilitation program.

Espinoza said, "During my career, I've learned and I've witnessed everything. I've been the highest of highest and lowest of the lowest, for me, it's just another challenge.

He returned back to horse racing in 2019. "Nothing is easy. This sport, it's always a challenge, but I like it. The challenge makes me focus more and try harder. "He's always kept himself in tip-top shape and says he's ready to move out the gate. He said, he's getting close to 49 but isn't thinking about retirement.

He also donates 10% of his winning to city of hope, a pediatric cancer research foundation. Victor Espinoza donated all of his Triple Crown winnings to charity. Espinoza will be following the lead of trainer Bob Baffert and donating his winnings to charity. The Baffert family will be donating $50,000 both to the permanently disabled Jockeys Fund and the California Retirement Management Account. Espinoza will direct his 80,000 dollar prize to California-based cancer research center.

Jose Espinoza got a chance to celebrate the Triple Crown victory with his brother. He couldn't stop hugging and loving on his brother.

(1.) Mama did manage to connect with a Firm in Dallas Texas. They will clear off all of her land and start building the horse Training Center. She drew up most of the blue prints herself to cut cost. They were very eager to work for Mama Faye.

(2.) The Disability Park for Horse Riding will also have a Huge Sensory Room, So they can spend the whole day on the ranch. She want the children to feel comfortable.

(3.) Mama still haven't heard from Tyler Perry. But she is still focus on her goals and being hopeful!

The Final Series

Introduction

<u>The 2017 Kentucky Derby</u> is the 143rd running on Saturday, May 6th, 2017. It's a horse race held each year in Louisville, Kentucky on the first Saturday in May. A grade 1 stakes race for 3 years old thoroughbreds at a distance of 1 ¼ **miles**, run at Church Hill Downs Race Track since its inception in 1875.

The National Weather Service estimates a 60% chance of rain in Louisville on Friday night, 40% chance of showers after 9 a.m. Saturday. It also included a 6:45 p.m. Derby Post Time of about 60 minutes; a 20-horse race. <u>Classic Empire</u>, along with <u>Always Dreaming</u>, was as of Tuesday the Vegas co-favorite at 4-1 and has raced just once on a sloppy track.

Over 150,000 people are expected to attend. The derby is significantly larger than other comparable sports events such as the Super Bowl, the World Series, or the NCAA Final Four. Are you in the mood for amusement? It's Mama's last derby party. Will she meet her goal? Will Tyler Perry connect with Mama? Will family secrets be revealed? Who is the glue for this party?

Sports Mom Final Series

Character List

<u>Mama Faye</u>- Still brainy and brave, she loves to entertain. She still loves going to the beauty shop and getting her nails done. She's always got something cooking on the stove.

<u>Betty Haris</u>- She's still bossy, lonely, and quite a flirt with those big bubbly eyes. She can be loud with a potty mouth. She finally gave up the spicy foods, but she still gets lost even with a GPS.

<u>Aunt Peaches</u>- She can be a little too energetic, loud, and all over the place. She's a blond now, and still sipping on White Lightning. She packed those short shorts for Derby Day; she's a cougar.

<u>Marlene Black</u> - She's still quiet and reserved with a low, raspy voice. She's really greying, and she has a habit of fidgeting at social gatherings. She just got back onto the dating scene.

<u>Uncle Bubba</u> - A.K.A. the Rib Burner, an inside joke. He's still absent minded, funny, quick-tempered, and dangerous on a grill. He loves to flirt, can be furious and suspicious, and is still cursing.

<u>Frederick</u>- A.K.A. Fred. He's Faye's son, a sneaky, messy boy who's always plotting something. He dresses casual with saggy jeans, and he's growing a goatee. The girls love his height -63" - and that he's dependable and fresh, but he's also known to be deceiving and shady.

<u>Bubba Wallace</u> – Professional NASCAR Driver Might Show up, We gatta Keep our hands Crossed.

Mama knows this is a horse derby party. But she wanted to invite one of her friends that also made history in 2013.

Bubba Wallace - a 27 year old, African American from Mobil Alabama made headlines in 2013, when he became the first African-American in 50 years to win one of Nascar's top 3 national touring series.

Bubba drives the No.23 Toyota Camry for the new Michael Jordan and Denny Hamlin owned 23XL racing team in the Nascar cup series the top racing circuit in America.

As a sports lone black drivers, Bubba has played a critical part in Nascar's push for inclusion and equality including its band of the confederate flag and races

Then in 2018, Bubba became a full-time driver in Nascar's premier cup series and proceeded to finish second in his first Daytona 500, again drawing headlines. He is considered one of the most successful African-American drivers in the history of Nascar, and he loves a tournament and competitiveness.

One of mama's favorite vacation spots back in the day was gulf shores in Alabama. There are plenty of restaurants shops activities and nightlife around the area. Back then she was a long haul truck driver. She dated one of his family members. The long distance relationship didn't work out. But, she still vacation. Sometimes reminiscing about her baby.

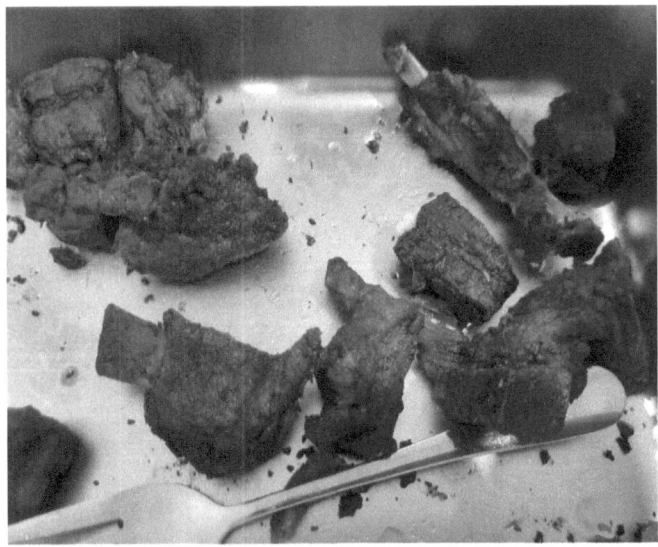

Uncle Bubba's Jacked up ribs, The sauce keep disappearing

Chapter 1

To start, it's around noon, and there's a light cloud in the sky and a lively feel to the place! Athens, Georgia, 65 miles northwest of Atlanta. City Hall, one of the highest points in Athens, is 761 feet above sea level. It's one of the most unique and memorable cities that exist.

Mama's two-story house is surrounded by a gorgeous garden. She's standing on the porch, viewing the Blue Ridge Mountains. She can smell the grass being mowed, and she can hear dogs barking and air planes flying over the house. She's usually somewhere daydreaming, but not today. Her honey skin tans too easily.

Meanwhile, Fred, cuts her a beautiful Bouquet of freesia flowers, bursting with fragrance. His red, bouncy, braided hair is always all over the place; his light skin and freckles always change in the sun. As he's pulling a bag of dirt to the porch, breathing hard, and sweating, "This dirt felt like a ton of bricks!" But he knows the smell of Mama's rose bushes gets everyone's attention.

Mama picked peaches earlier today, so she and Fred are on the porch, enjoying their sweet peaches Tammy stole some peaches in front of everybody and ran. After that, Gracie, Fred's cat, jumped onto Frederick and licked his peach; her personality is just like his messy. Fred grabbed Mama's hand and said, "Come on. Let's sit at the dining room table." After moving, he asked, "What's up, Mama? You haven't been yourself lately. Your anxiety and panic attacks are off the chain."

Mama, looking stressed, said, "Initially, like I mentioned in February, I got the devastating news from Janetta; she can't host the party this year! The water crisis in Flint, Michigan has gotten worse. Son! I'm really stressed out and falling apart..." "Mama!" Fred said, I got you! I've been working on some surprises for the party. Don't worry about the food. This will be the most memorable Derby Party you've ever had. Sylvester (A.K.A. 'Little Shorty!") is helping since his dad Mr. Father Ruben, the Amish priest) will be out of town. Shorty's bringing grilled goat ribs, and his mom's dropping off stuffed Amish hog maws. Gee!"

Additionally, Bubba's on board and making extra food. She teared up but felt relieved and said, "Give me a hug! I'm so proud of you." He winked and said, "Love you, mom!" She went upstairs, and Fred immediately started emptying boxes and decorating. Shorty's at the door. Fred said, "What's up, cuz? We got about 3 hours of work to do." "Eew" shorty exclaimed, "Glad I got zooted before coming. It turns me into a workaholic, but keep teaching me 'slang' and street talk. You're a good teacher Fred. Thanks!

Meanwhile, Mama's still upstairs, trying on hats and clothes. She's sipping some Ciroc Vodka to help soothe her pain. She started daydreaming and fell asleep. She slept for 3 hours but was feeling real good, that motown music just sets her on fire. She thought, I need me a boyfriend before I turn into a malfunctional drunk, but what they don't know won't hurt.

Downstairs, Shorty told Fred, "I'm glad the Priest is out of town at a convention. He's clothed in Amish religion." Fred asked him, "Yo! Cuz! You gonna grill one of his goats?" "yeah, I'm tired of feeding them, and besides, I'm raising them goats! Haha!"

But, let me tell you what he did in Ohio. This is inhuman and will make you sick. A lady accidentally ran over one of his crows/ He had a hissy fit. Cremated and buried him. Then took the lady to court. Fred declared, he is beyond mental and shook his head.

"What is all this stuff?" Beistle Horse Racing Cover with plates to match, red and gold balloons, plastic jockey helmets to go on tables, western cowgirl dessert plates, and mint julep glasses. After observing it all, Fred said, "Dude! This is overkill! Well, let's check out these cakes that Mama made." These consisted of a Derby turtle cake, a Bishop's cake, a chocolate prune cake, and a rabbit pie. "Eew! I thought it's against the law to eat a Bishop's cake?" Shorty asked, and Fred replied, Cuz! Not at this party. What you mean?"

Wait until you see what Peaches whips up. Touch My Soul!' That's hilarious, and she's one crazy lady!" Fred said, then Shorty changed the subject, saying "So, cuz! I got good news. I go to jockey school in July. I met all of the qualifications; I'm the right height, weight, experience, but I have to take a physical. I hope they don't notice my missing index finger". "Don't worry about that, cuz!" Fred reassured, and joked, "You gonna have to start taking daily showers. You can't be standing by a horse smelling like a goat. You know that horse will run off, and you will never see him again!"

"Huh!" Shorty started, "I've been working with horses all my life and never heard of such a thing. I'll get it before the Priest comes home."

Fred had a blank stare and said, "Cuz! You gonna be alright. Let's talk about the race. Cuz! I'm putting $200 on Looking at Lee." "Eew! Why cuz?" Shorty asked, and Fred told him, "He likes to ride hard and dirty like me." Shorty said, "I'm going with Classic Empire. He's a favorite and a come-from-behind horse like me. I'm betting $50 on him."

Next, while Mama's walking down the stairs, she was ear-jacking. She shouted, "Beautiful! Fantastic! The flowers and decorations all go together. Y'all did a wonderful job!" "Thanks, Mama!" Fred stated. Shorty stated, "I got to roll before they start blowing my phone up," Shorty told them, and Fred said, "Cuz! I'm hitting the sack, too. Got a long day tomorrow at Bubba's. I don't know what kinda mood he's gonna be in, but I can't wait to get on his computer. He never logs out unless it's Lowes. Haha!"

Fred is up early with the sunrise. He goes down stairs and notice Mama has pasted every horses story on poster board. They have individual stories. She has decorated them like a graphic design artist. Each horse has it's on personality. Fred said, Wild! Mama! I love this. Did you stay up all night? Nah!

- She wanted everyone to get familiar with their horse picks. The horses refused to be left outta this party. They have been trash-talking, on the way to their gates. Inside their gates, and during the race. Its A Wrap!

They all will get animated with each other before the race starts.

Chapter 2

At this time, early Friday morning, there's lots of rain and fog. Mama just woke up; she slept like a baby. All of the ladies have arrived except Marlene - it takes her 3 hours to put on makeup. Mama's killing two birds with one stone!' She's making breakfast and brunch at the same time. This food should last until midnight! Oh! My! The smell of coffee and cinnamon rolls is breathtaking.

Here's a list of the good stuff Mama is making: Rodeo hash, Lickety-split biscuits, Wagon Wheel Sausage pie. Million Dollar pie, Baked Polish omelets, A Rebel's Devilled grits, Bible School punch and Republican pie. Betty's like no thanks! I am a Democrat.

While Betty is at the table drinking coffee, Marlene pulls into the driveway. She enters the house, and something smells spicy. With a hoarse voice, Betty looks at her watch and asks, "Why are you so late?" Marlene giggled and said, "Child, Robert was riding me like a white horse! I almost didn't make it." They all had a good laugh. Mama said, "Come on, and let's eat." Peaches said, "These grits are scrumptious!"

Subsequently, Fred is up! He got cleaned up, made himself a to-go plate, and drove to Bubba's house, who lives in the rural Athens, Georgia, a very remote-feeling place. It's 60 degrees and a bit hazy with a humid atmosphere. He lives 15 minutes from downtown. Lots of zit-popping teenagers are around, and college students hang out in local bars. Jittery Joe's Coffee Shop is Bubba's hangout. The town is bike-friendly and has free public transportation.

His house is surrounded by paved ground with various party spots, plus babbas fancy barbeque fire pit. Sadly a few years ago, Bubba burned down the whole pit to the ground in his back yard. People are still wondering how it happened, and some come by and take pictures like it's some monument. Bubba has been up since 6 a.m. prepping his foods for Saturday. His menu consists of these:

McDaddy mac and cheese, 10-Slabs Cola-and-Coffee beef ribs, 6-slabs Chili-and-Mustard baby backs, 3 Grilled Chicken on the run, and Mexican Windy City grilled corn. He's in a good mood, blasting his blues music. Some of his favorites are B.B.King, Washboard Sam, Johnny Taylor, Big Mama Thornton, Muddy Waters, and Lead Belly.

Someone is banging on Bubba's door like crazy! Bubba says, "Who is it?" When there was no answer, he panicked, went upstairs, got his Glock 27, and opened the door. "Yo, cuz!" Fred yelled and asked, "What are you doing? Are you alright? Who you got beef with?" When Bubba told him no one, Fred demanded, "Go put that gun up! Right on! Right on!"

Bubba told him, "You're late! I thought you were coming early this morning" Fred said, "I was, but I ran into one of my foxes. She talked me into getting a room. You know I couldn't turn that down! A red-bone, too," he said, smiling big and wide.

Fred exclaimed "sit down, cuz! We got to talk." Shorty just pulled up in the yard and came in, saying, "Hey! What's up? Fred tells Bubba the good news. Now, we have a special guests coming to the party. He's a relative." Bubba asked, "Why are you telling me?" "Because he's your nephew, Yussef". A stand up comedian. "Who?" "Your folks, cuz!" Bubba turned red in the face and said, "I haven't heard from him in 9 years how'd you contact that nut, huh?" And shorty replied, he seen last year's sports video online it went viral." Ok! I got a joke!

Bubba said, "Listen both of you come here there's a tree stump in Louisiana swamp with a higher IQ than Yussef's!" Eew! Good grief! Shorty almost wet his pants laughing, saying," "Wild, cuz! Crap happens." Bubba asks, "So, where is Yussef staying?" to which Fred replied, "With you, for 3 days. I'm picking him up at 11 p.m. tonight." Bubba said, exasperated, "A bad penny always show up! Okay! Three days is all I can take of Yussef. And don't have him frustrating Mama. You know she has bipolar disorder." Fred, wide-eyed, red in the face and shocked said I thought all of this stuff with mama is normal! Nah! Faye is a little touched and it's not by an angel. Hahaha! Fred said don't go there Dawg, We'll be here all night talking about your issues right on!

Fred said my thoughts are off the charts about mama. Uncle Bubba I think mama used to be a moonshiner back in the day. Bubba replied, what makes you think that? Ughh! She knows too much about them and every time I turn around someone is always bringing her a jar to sample and she start naming off ingredients and numbers you know she's the jack of all trades so why would I scratch this off the list shorty said maybe you're on rabbit trail.

Bubba interjected, I plead the fifth. You going to have to talk to Faye about that, you feel me? Fred said yeah! I felt that! Fred thought, I think both of them was in the moonshine Business. Plus mama was a grave digger. You know they hang around the cemeteries pouring white lightning on their Friends graves. Fred immediately had a Flash Back, when I was around 8 years old. Old Bubba would always take me up in the woods. They all had on overalls and suspenders and it would always be near a water supply. Bubba just joined in, cuzz! It looked like some type of science Fair. Shorty said, seriously! Bubba's rubbing off on you! Nah! But, to illustrate mama was pulled over on the back road. The Cop checked her information, then mama popped the trunk and gave him a Mason Jar of moonshine, and we were on our way. Now, I get it. Shorty said, I need a Jar so I can spike the Priest's Coffee every morning. He is so deep into his religion, he would never know the difference. Yikes!

Fred asked why is he always riding a taxi or uber? Shorty came out with the dignified Priest can't drive a car, he just want to be glorified, and keep living in the 1950's. Someone need to give him some parenting classes. I doubt if he can even read that bible he carry around, Fred said, he need to FALL BACK! They laughed it off.

Fred later said, a Priest should have a bachelor's degree. Must study Philosophy and religion. Must attend seminary for 5 years. Shorty cracked his side laughing, stating that the religion is the only box I can check off, he's swamped in religion.

In fact the priest put me in front of the church to be shunned. Then you are separated from your community, socialization, family and friends. For a while, what a dumb law.

I questioned how could a church leader, or priest be "right-next to God." Then I said where is Jesus gonna sit? They immediately shunned me, "I'm tired of dealing with these Dip sticks! Fred replied Darn!

Chapter 3

After finding out about Mama, Fred thought they should have told me before daddy died, saying, "Mama could've told me" feeling deceived, caught off guard. His heart is beating fast, non-stop; he's trying to calm down. Shorty called him to the car so they could get zooted, telling him, "Here, bruh! Take a hit. "That weed mellowed him out, and Fred said, "Okay, thanks cuz! Let's go back inside. I got some more questions." Shorty's home grown weed. Got me looking cockeyed.

Bubba took him a shot of White Lightning from his mason jar. They are all sitting in the living room. So Fred uttered, "if I'm a psychopath, Bubba got personality disorder or O.C.D." Shorty implied the whole family is disturbed. Bubba replied,"Y'all got the wrong man. Ain't nothing wrong with me! I'm cleared by the doctor. Peaches proclaimed, you both got something mental going on due to the ramifications of y'all's genes."

In retrospect, that explains Mama's mood swings. She's always up and down, and she's sometimes extremely irritable. That's why she retired from her state job and from grave digging. Bubba babbled and pulled out his sympathy card, wanting to encourage Fred, "I'm sorry for your hurt and pain. I thought your parents told you." "Nah!" Fred exclaimed and said, "I just thought it was due to Mama's hot flashes. That's all she talks about." Bubba told him, "I'm always here for you," and Fred said, "I know, Uncle. You can get real crazy sometimes. I'm gonna be alright. I'm gonna start going on her appointments."

"Right on!" Bubba spoke, "Hey! Tell your boy Little Shorty he need to make sure he bathe before coming to the party. He can't be around me smelling like no Billy goat! Now, eew that!" he said, and they both laughed so loud. "Haha!"

So, on Friday, mid-morning at Bubba's, Fred said, "Cuz!I got to roll! I have to touch base with these citizens to make sure they bring food tomorrow." Bubba told him, "Right on! But please occupy Yussef when he gets here and while I'm grilling. Take him sight-seeing or woman-hunting, and keep it legal! "Alright, cuz!" Fred said. Bubba's checking his vegetable garden and preparing to go fishing at Cat Creek, his favorite place to fish.

Meanwhile, the rain has cleared up at Mama's, and the aroma in her kitchen is breathtaking. All the ladies are individually preparing their foods, Peaches said, "Too many cooks spoil the broth!" sipping on May Flower martini's all day. Some of their potlucks look like this:

Peaches is making:
Oven chicken feet and rice
Bacon and bourbon Collards
Derby Turtle Cake

Betty is making:
Kiss pie- for Bubba
Funeral Mashed Potatoes
Walking Tacos

Marlene is making:
Bourbon bread pudding
Uncle Rain's Gospel chicken
A Pack of Wild corndogs

However, the UPS driver just delivered a dozen of red and white roses to Mama. She can't believe her eyes! She asked the driver, "Who sent these?" and he replied, "Not me! I can't afford roses. Well, have a good day, ma'am." Peaches took the roses and sat Mama down, giving her a glass of water. Thanks," Mama told her, "I'm hot flashing like a yellow traffic light." They were all elated at the roses. The sender was unknown. Peaches insisted, "Who's the secret guy you haven't told us about?" I'm puzzled, too," Mama told her.

At present, Friday night, Fred just walked into Bubba's house. The TV has been blasting for a few hours on his favorite reality show, Live P.D.! With blue, flashing lights, sirens are all over the TV. You can hear it 31 blocks away. Bubba is knocked out in his recliner with the front door wide open. His Labrador retriever, Buddy, is laying right next to him on the floor.

Fred though, this is disgusting. Buddy got more sense than Bubba does. These blue lights is driving me crazy. Fred turned off the TV, woke Bubba up, and gave him his medication, telling him, Come on, cuz! Let me help you to your bedroom." He also put Buddy in the room with him and closed the door.

In the meantime, he got on Bubba's computer and thought, he only log out when he buys grills online from Lowes. Wait! What is this? Huh! Farmersonly.com. This is a dating site. Wild! This dude is nuts, LA Paris and JaJie, two gold diggers, LA Paris looking like she could be a man in drag. I know Bubba is all man, but sometimes he doesn't pay close attention. I'm gonna let him deal with this mess, my lips are sealed! Next, Fred looks down in the trash can, containing lots of balled-up papers. He pulled one out and read it, 'Bubba Jones banned from all Taco Bells in Georgia for disorderly conduct.' Huh! Fred thought, I wonder what he did? A senior getting banned from Taco Bell is never ludicrous. Let me dig a little more! Fred just emptied out the can, finding a Bosley Hair Restoration order, assuming Bubba was going bald on top. He's ordered his kit, and it's on the way. He shook his head and thought, he's a looney bin! Ignorance can be educated, crazy can be medicated. But there is no cure for stupid. Fred laugh to himself.

Chapter 4

Now, it's time to pick up Yussef from the airport. They met in baggage claims. Fred spotted him a mile away. He's the tallest person in the airport. "Hey! Cuz, how was your flight from Detroit?" Fred asked, It was smooth and nice. They moved me up to first class because of my height. I sat next to a fox! She was fine as wine." Fred asked, "Did you get them digits?"Bruh! You know I did, and she lives in Grand Rapids, Michigan. But cuz! I heard you were brainy, bull-headed, and bitter." "I was a preteen when you left. I remember that scar behind your ear." Well! It's permanent." "Did you get darker?" Yeah!" Yussef said, and Frederick tells him, "I heard you speak 3 different languages," and Yussef replies, "I do; I wanted to be a foreign service officer.

Yussef tells him, "Playing minor league baseball in Florida gives you a permanent tan. My coach in high school told me I was gifted in playing first base and catching. I caught for Aroldis Chapman, relief pitcher of the New York Yankees, when we played in the Netherlands. I drove the getaway car to help him defect to the airport. When the Cincinnati Reds called him up, I was still in Florida in minor leagues, waiting to get called up. Chapman told them I was his catcher. I never heard from MLB. Major League Baseball. I'm finally over it.

Likewise, Bubble told me. "They spooked you, you panicked and started acting crazy down there, and you blew your chance of ever going into the major leagues." Yussef became enraged, and he shouted, Get out! You walk home! Cuz, this is my ride!" Concerned, Fred asked, "You alright?" "Yeah man." I'm sorry. I lost my head! What just happened'?" Yussef asked, and Fred told him, "You went crazy for a minute." He told Fred, "I'm straight now." Bruh! All of us might have mental disorders. Nah! Them your folks. I'm the chosen one cuz!

They finally pulled up at Bubba's house. They enter the house, and Live P.D. Reality TV is blasting again. "Bruh! Who is watching this show? Who is trying to get lit up with blue lights at 2 a.m.? "Yussef questioned. Fred tells him, "Cuz! I swear, this TV was off when

I left." Yussef says, Bruh! Sound like some ghost might be living here, too. Maybe that's who's hiding his grills" They both grinned.

Hey Cuz! You want a drink?" Fred offered, and Yussef replied, "Yeah! So what's Bubba been doing?" He sits in Bubba's chair, and Fred tells him, "Let that recliner all the way back. You'll definitely like it." Yussef asks, "When did he start burning up ribs and grills?" "Since I was in 3rd grade," Fred tells him, He went through about 30 grills my whole childhood. It was gas grills, electric, and charcoal. And he always blamed me for his shortcomings. Now, he's blaming it on the neighborhood kids. This dude can be mean, miserable, and moody! Any little thing can trigger him, especially when he hears the word grill. He needs a woman bad" "Oops!" "He only gets 3 Viagra pills a month," and Yussef asks, "For what?" Haha!

Fred continues, "Then last year, he bought an $800 grill, burned up 12 slabs of meat in it, and started a grill fire. The fire department came once more and put it out. They gave him a $500 fine. I have no idea where he puts them afterwards, He has every Grillmaster Certificate for the state of Georgia. He's got them plastered all over his office wall, Sure, I wish I had the key" Yussef asks, "Bruh! Where is he getting the money from" and Fred announced, "Retirement check, Social. Security, Pension, and they need to give him a Crazy Check. He's very neglectful and compulsive, he has 3 of everything!" Yussef said, "Bruh! And he talking about I'm a nut! Really! "Tell it to the marines!"

Now, it's Saturday morning: Derby Day. Bubba, who's just taken his meds, has been up since 5 a.m. It's cloudy outside, but just right for BBQ. He's got every piece of meat on the grill. Fred's up in the kitchen, starting breakfast: Black Pepper grits, Saucy Breakfast casserole, Beer biscuits, and Daquiri fruit salad. Someone have to get the ball rolling!

Yussef is lying in bed, thinking, sweating, and turning pale. He thought, I'm worried about this senior audience. I'm out of my league! I don't have any senior-fresh material. What if they reject me? The heat is on; this could be devastating, disastrous, and deadly for me. I'm feeling uncertain, so I do need to research those Derby horses. I can wing it on the rest. "Being that I'm a Stand up Comic, I usually write my own material. I can't even write a paragraph, my brain won't give me anything. Not even a crumb."

He cleaned up and headed to the kitchen, and he said, "Bruh! I'm ready to throw down. I'm as hungry as a horse!" They're eating, catching up on small talk. Bubba said, "We're leaving at 2 p.m. sharp headed to Mama's house." Fred said, "Bubba, can you please not wear that dumb tee shirt?" Which one?" Bubba asks, and Fred tells him, "The one with Kiss My Bass' on the back." "Sorry! I already ironed it." "But Bubba! You're gonna look like a 'poop head!' Right on!"

Bubba is finishing his BBQ in the front yard. Fred and Yussef are checking the burned -down pit in the back yard. Yussef lifted the lid from the ground and said, "Holy smoke! It smells like a skunk was living here. This shed! "Cuz! I've got the keys," Fred opened the shed. What a discovery! Burned up grills from the present and years ago were all stacked on top of each other! Some of these looked familiar to Fred, then he said, "Wait, this one still got the burned-up bones in it, Inhuman and demonic! The smoker to this one is detached. Why are the nails and screws burned up on this one? This one is a gas grill, looks like it just blew up in the yard" I'm surprised they haven't cut off his Government Checks yet. A perfect example of grill abuse.

Yussef commented, "It's 50 grills in here! Why didn't he take them to the junk yard? "Fred says, "He was too embarrassed. Would you help him load up the grills and take them to the junk yard" Yussef replied, "Nah! But he's still shady and scandalous. He's wondering why he ain't got no woman. He need a nursing home, bruh! Somebody need to buy him some brains!"

"Let's roll" Yussef says, put the keys away. They left Bubba in the yard barbecuing. You can tell Bubba's getting drowsy, trying to stay awake, fighting it hard. Finally, he's asleep. The grill top is down, but something is flaming and burning underneath. Smoke went everywhere for 2 hours, and finally, nuts and bolts started falling off. By now, the neighbor Ulyssess called the fire department for the 30th time.

Fred and Yussef are 3 blocks from the house, and the smell of burned meat is electric in the air. Fred says I've seen this movie before, all of the birds are flocking to it. Lucky is trying to wake him, shouting! "Hey pops! This lucky man, wake up! Fred jumped out of the car and talks to the fire chief, the chief explained, "Look man! This old dude needs help. We're tired of putting out grill fires. It's too risky for him. Why is he always falling asleep" Fred tells him, "Cuz! I've been trying to figure it out myself" Fred said, I've begged him to give up the grill.

He refused too. Chief said, Maybe we can slap some Felony charges on him. Fred vented, Nah! Mama knows all of Law enforcement up to the President. Seriously!

Then the chief tells Fred that Bubba now needs constant supervision while grilling, and tells him, "He's already gotten 3 warnings, huh! This is the last one. One more call, and he will be lit up with blue lights." Fred jokes, saying, "He might like that. All he watch is cop shows and Live P.D. (off the record!)". The guy asks him, Does he have a sleeping disorder?" and Fred replies, "Officer, it's too deep for me to get into." Officer tells Fred, "You do know that grill he just burned up costs $572 at Lowes, right?" Huh!" Fred exclaimed, saying, "I didn't know he was spending that type of money!" Well," the chief states, I'm leaving. Keep an eye on old dude."

After the all-clear sign and the lid cooling off, they tried opening the lid. The hinges fell off, what a devastation. A few bolts and screws fell to the ground, there was a screeching sound, and the black knobs were melted to a crisp. The whole grill collapsed. You could hear the sizzle form the burned meat. The atmosphere is set, the vultures', buzzards, pheasants and woodpeckers are ready to eat.

The 10 slab of pork ribs were burned to the bones. No mercy for them! The 6 slabs of baby backs in the smoker side were overcooked. The rub charred up, and the water pan was dry as a desert. Yussef said, "Mama's gonna have a cow!" "Shut up! Fred warned him. Bubba said, "We take 4 slabs of baby backs and pull the meat off of 2 slabs. I'll throw it in the baked beans for a smoky taste. So, now the problem is solved." He asks, "What's more important? The 10 slabs of pork ribs or the baby backs?" and Fred tells him, "Cuz! Nevertheless, all 16 slabs won't be accounted for, Bubba said, Fred you're an unreasonable Jive Turkey.

They are loading up the foods for Mama's house. Yussef is picking up grill pieces, throwing them onto the wheelbarrow, and taking them to the back yard. He is snapping pictures like crazy with his camera phone, Bubba walked up behind him and says, "Hey, fool! What you doing?" Yussef replied, "Oh! I wanted pictures for my scrapbook." Angry, Bubba says heck no! You punk! Go help Fred. "Fred tells him, "Come on, man."Yussef was hot, saying, "Hey man, you need to get your uncle.

He's gonna make me lay him down! Trying to diffuse him, Fred says, "Cuz! Don't pay him any attention, He's an old fart!" Just Iike his Neighbor down the street, Mr. August, He's Meddlesom, Moody, and a mobster. Yussef' said, what's wrong with this old man? I've seen him 3 days straight. Walking up and down the street with no shirt on in 90° weather. He just might be a terrorist. Fred said. Yep! I feel you Bruh! But wait until you see his monster truck.

Mr. August Monster Truck

Mama went to school with Mr. August and Tanner, Bubba's always said both of them have 2 loose screws. He hate's Mr. August because he's always Snapping Pic's when his grills blow up. He has tons of photos, I've seen them. All on his flip phone.

"Later on Yussef, I will tell you about his pet owl named Chili!"

Fred states. Uncle Bubba hates Tanner's guts because Mama made him the back-up grill master. Bubba says, he has no clout, anyone can do a pig roast.

Firstly, he cuts the pigs head off after grilling. He then put them in his freezer until Halloween. He put the heads on broom handles and scare the kids during Halloween. What! you can't make this stuff up!

Secondly, the neighborhood kids want nothing to do with him. Plus Bubba want to put a slug in him and end it all. It's too many weirdos in the town.

Yussef added, I was on my morning run. Mr. August was sitting on his poarch and stopped me. He informed me about Chili, the owl, who knows his face and voice. He feeds him mounds chocolate bars.

"Fred commented, don't the feather brain know they can't process sugar?" Nah, He has dark sinister eyes, made me nervous. How do you'll put up with the goof? Fred's like according to the priest he's labeled immoral and impure. "Hahaha! Keep An Eye on Them Both!"

Fred also said, Mr. August is also known to sprinkle some salt on the priest steps. Huh!

Chapter 5

Fred is using cruise control going to Mama's house, running late. He tells Bubba, "Consequently, got to break you these news. The fire chief said you can't BBQ anymore without grill supervision.

He said this was your 30th warning, and it's the last one. He said you're a 'flight risk!" Bubba turned red, mad as a wet hen!

He felt affronted, so he yelled and snapped, cursing out Fred and Yussef! Everything went silent for a second, then Bubba let out a big burp without covering his mouth. Fred and Yussef mumbled, "Seriously! Shenanigan!" They both couldn't wait to get to Mama's house. Bubba said, ""Don't tell me nothing else that fire chief said, and you can tell him to Kiss My Bass!" They all laughed so hard. Bubba then stated, This Tee-Shirt Talks for me. Haha!

Fred pulled up in Mama's driveway. They thought it was a block party. You could hear the music 3 blocks away. Just what the seniors ordered! Motown, The Temptations, and Four Tops. Shorty's in the driveway. Looking outta place, and shaking two dice in his hands.

"What's crackin'?" Fred asked. Shorty announced, "Y'all are late!" He told him, "Bubba had another grill fire." "Eew! A leopard can't change its spots!" And Bubba asks, "What did you say? "Oops!" "Boy, you lucky I ain't got my hearing aid. I will snatch a knot in your rear!" Shorty had a dead look on his face.

At this moment, Yussef went inside, saying, "Mama, you looking gorgeous!" to which she replied, "Thanks! I ran into your kids at Popeye's chicken. I can't believe Yadira's 10-and Yoenis is 6-years-old already! They have really grown up. They told me you were in town."Yussef told her, "Yes, I'm the comedian for your party." "Oh boy!" she shouted and said, "Fred told me he had some surprises. Well, make yourself at home." Right away, he made himself familiar with his environment and the pre-game activities, as always.

Everyone is talking and defending their horses for this race. Most think it will be a tight race. You can't always go by their odds and the sports analysts. The 24-hour horse channel has been on since Thursday, Fred can't wait until this party is over! He thinks he might have O.C.D Disorder from watching mama's 24-hour horse Channel, four days Straight.

The pre-game activities consist of live horseshoe throwing, Million Dollars/Rooster Teeth board game, Crash! The Bankrupt game, The Farming Game, Ghettopoly, Monopoly, card games, and chess, all along with the Motown music. Some drinking consists of Thunderbird, Jonnie Walker, White Tennessee wine, Old Milwaukee, and Schlitz beers. Someone also put 2 mason jars of White Lightening on the drink table. "Straight Outta Georgia Woods!"

Mr. August is driving up and down the street in his raggedy monster truck making noise. He uses a step ladder and cane to get in it. Tanner vented, last Wednesday he had the Community looking for Lad his dog. Mr. August shared, no sign of him. He invited Tanner in for a drink. Tanner sat on the couch then blabbered, what's that foul smell? Smell like a dead beaver. Mr. August didn't smell anything. Tanner turned up the Mason Jar of Moonshine. Tanner went to the guest bathroom, and screamed! Bruh! Here's your dead dog. He got into rat poison, been here for 5 days. Mr. August had down cast eyes. Tanner ran all the way home, then called Animal Control. What a head case.

Bubba walked in and went straight to the card table where Betty, his secret crush, was playing. She looked up at Bubba with her large, deep-set, bulging eyes. She couldn't stop blinking, so one of her lashes fell off. Bubba got down underneath the table and found it, and when he attempted to put it back on for her, he accidentally kissed her. She loved it, so he stuck his tongue down her throat! Shorty shouted, "Get a room!" and everyone cracked up laughing! But Bubba's shirt is really standing out. Fernando asked Fred, "Is he alright?" and he replied, "I doubt it, bruh!"

Most of the guys are in the 'man cave,' watching TV on the 75" Samsung screen. Yussef is taking his time, writing mini notes. His worrying is becoming a panic and crisis, and he's thinking, how did I get myself into this mess? Will this fear follow me to the stage?

He was approaching some food tables and thinks, you'll keep it 100 up in here. Who bring this kind of food to a horse party? Who are these community people? A bunch of weirdos, individualists, and misfits! They got me feeling frail and frantic, not to mention all of these demons on my back! I don't remember none of these folks. Imma have to hit a shot of that white lightening before I hit the stage. I need to turn up!

In turn, Mama just came back downstairs. She just had her another shot and is turnt-up! She announced, "The comedian will come to the stage in 1 hour." Yussef gasped and thought, great! Now I can run downstairs and use the bathroom in peace. When he arrived, Marlene was blowing it up. Yikes! It smelled deadly. It had to be that sardine casserole or them Montana mountain beans. They done been told to stay out of them mountains! These folks is from the Wilderness.

Peaches is drunk as a skunk on the balcony! Without her teeth, she's cursing out her boyfriend, and she's giving him the business. She done turnt up and down! She's not in any shape to be watching the derby or comedy Show, ughh! What did Peaches put on him? Some Snap Back!

Bubba is still flirting with Betty. He did manage to get a date before she leaves. He needs a woman bad. Maybe he can get his Viagra increased and stop burning up grills! Haha! Yussef said, them kinda pills don't work on Bubba. Shorty said, watcha mean? Bubba is an old Coon, with super low energy. Shorty replied, Pimpin Aint Eazy!

Fernando was confused about the writing on the back of Bubba's shirt "Kiss My Bass!" Fred answered, It's a long story Hoomie. We can make a lunch date. Fernando had a Quirky Voice, Seriously! But your uncle is a wackadoo! Fred stated the whole community is like that, a bunch of hippies and maniacs.

Bubba has been thinking about Yussef story. It don't make sense, I had a buddy who stayed in the minor leagues for 10 years, and finally got called up to the major leagues. Yussef is sorry, lazy and creepy. I think he just went to the college to chase down women. I can't listen to anymore of his baseball lies. I want to slice him up like a pound cake.

"Horse Drama at Church Hill Downs"

Position:	Name:	Odds:
#1	<u>Looking At Lee</u>	28-1

I've had 6 straight races; I love running on a sloppy track hard! Hence touched my tail and it feels so scummy! Then he had the nerve to say to me, "Stop whining!" "So just keep on looking at me! I've never bitten off more than I can chew!" Then, he passed gas, and The smell was a definite blast from the past.

#2	<u>Thunder Snow</u>	16-1

You can't steal my thunder! I've raced all over the world: England, Dubai, even Europe! My owner is a Prime Minister, so I've got "Favor!" Always Dreaming said, "You tried to throw your owner off of your back!" I said, "You been ear hustlin' again? Tryin' to jack my conversation?" Always dreaming simply said, "Horse, bye!" and trotted off!

#3	<u>Fast and Accurate</u>	66-1

"Oops! Yikes! I've got the hiccups! I'm P.H.A.T.! (Pretty, Hot, and Tempting) I've won two stakes on that turf track! My command is like Major League Pitcher's, David Price! "Fast, accurate, and on point!" A famous empire once said, "Beauty is only skin deep!" And I thought to myself, "I know! Duh!?

#4	<u>Untrapped</u>	50-1

The crowd is loud! The funnel clouds of track dirt are making me depressed. I'm feeling a little defeated. I ran 3d in both the Indiana and Ohio Derbies. I had the lead, but those dudes said, "You're too scared to pass the other horses!" "You think you move great, but you don't! You're a lame! And you have no talent! You qualified for this race how?" So, I trotted up to Hence and held my head up tall, with my back straight and my tail high in the air... Bumping him on the nose, I said, "Don't make me go old School on you, PUNK!"

#5   <u>Always Dreaming</u>   4-1

I'm the real favorite in this race! This is not a dream!"
"My time was 36 in the Florida Derby. It was a 3/8 mile; ain't no stopping me now! My energy is too high! I ran so fast that I put my feet down on the gas! I started singing 'Burn Baby, Burn!' as I flew over that finish line!"

#6   <u>State Of Honor</u>   40-1

I high-tail it like Julio Jones does on a wet track! You'll honor me! Bow down before me when I win this race!" I run in a bar shoe to protect myself from damaging my hoof any further. Got 3 wins under my belt! The challengers are of no consequence to me! Red beans and rice fuel my speed! Sorry 'bout the droppings, by the way!" Oh! Fiddle sticks!"

#7   <u>Garvin</u>   16-1

I'm a longshot! I know! But I love this post! I've had a bit of surgery on my right front hoof, so I, too, will be wearing a bar shoe to protect my hoof. Got 3 wins under my belt, so I ain't new to the winner's circle. Carrots help my eyesight, and Golden Delicious apples make my coat shiny! So I've left droppings! But they don't stink!

#8   <u>Hence</u>   22-1

(Signing and humming) "Shoot! What was that? I just stepped on a cat's tail! Thank God I'm no superstitious!" The cat screeched and ran away. I almost threw my jockey. I won both the Iowa and Sunland Derbies. I love chillin' and getting my zoot on before a race! "I know I'm a hot mess! Tell me something I don't already know!"

#9   <u>Irag</u>   25-1

"I dominated the Indiana Derby! I was like a wild bear! A beast on that track! I ran past everyone, leavin' them all in my dust!" "They said I was doing the most in the Sunland Derby. I had a funky attitude; could be, because I drank a lot of vinegar. But don't play with me! I'm a pimp, at the top of my game! I'm about to have a New York minute up in this post!

#10   Gunnevera   12-1

"I'm the longshot everyone's forgotten about! You forgot about me! But don't sleep on me!" "I've shown well against Always Dreaming and Irish War Cry in the Gulf Stream Park Race. Always Dreaming told me to "Shut up! Go back to Skid Row!" But I said, yo shut up! That's no way to speak to a lady!" But then I got mad, and I started rapping <u>DMX Song</u>:

"Yall gon' make me lose my mind,
Up in here, up in here
Y all gon' make me go all out
Up in here, up in here...
Don't make me act a fool...
Up in here, up in here!"
Then, they backed up off of me.

#11   <u>Battle of Midway</u>   28-1

I've been just chillin' in my man cave. I never raced as a 2 yr. old! I win on wet, fast tracks. I won in Santa Anita by 3 lengths. I was feeling myself that day! I have 4 lifetime races under my belt." Hence said, "It's a dirty, lowdown shame! But you're gonna lose this race! AIright, alright, alright! You gone learn today!

#12   <u>Sonneteer</u>   50-1

What's crack-a-lackin'? Somebody jacked up my odds! These people are crazy! I'm so hungry, my belly thinks my throat's been cut!" Patch said, boringly, "You're winless in your last 10 starts!" and just shook his head! But Sonneteer stood proudly saying, "That's in my past, my backstory! But when this race starts, I'l be like Major League pitcher, Aroldis Chapman, that Cuban Misile Flame Thrower! 105 fast ball velocity!! In the final stretch, I'm gonna leave you in my dust! See you in your dreams!" Then, I trotted off.

#19   <u>Pratical Joke</u>   16-1

Google, quit actin' like you know everything! But then again, you may be a bit smarter than a caveman! Hahaha!" "On the other hand, you don't know jack about Jill" All the other horses started heeing and hawing. Then Patch said stupidly, "Who is Jack? Who is Jill? What an idiot!

#20   <u>Patch</u   33-1

"They think I'm the stupid one of the bunch, but little
do they know, I'm the favorite of them all!" "You see,
they're sleeping on me! I play dumb, but it is a defense
mechanism to get them thinking about one of the other
horses." "You see, even though I lost my left eye to an
ulcer, I sharpened my other senses and increased my
speed on em." They've got two good eyes, but they
won't see me comin'" "My trainer is upset that I won't
wear my blinders, but that shows weakness! And I'm
far from being weak! My handicap will never define
who I am! I'm gonna show up and show out!" "The
rain makes me sleepy, but I'm ready to roll in the deep!
So when I win, I'm gonna take my patch off in the
winners' circle for the whole world to see! Ah! The
sweet smell of rain, roses, and success! No weapon form
against me shall prosper!"

<u>Gormley</u> is having a few behavioral problems; he's being
stubborn. They all hate the noisy crowds. The horses are
all trash-talking at their post. Thunder Snow said, "Yuck!
Something stink in this gate. Smell like a dead buzzard"
State of Honor said, "Shut up! Your breath is kicking!"
Thunder Snow slapped State of Honor in the face with
his tail while they loaded into the gate, saying "Did you
hear the call to post, jerk?" "No" It's not time yet fool!
Plus I gotta pray!

Time For The Race:

In the meantime, everyone is gathered around a television with their favorite drinks in hand. They were frantic and on edge. Fred's cat Gracie got scared and ran away too much noise. Everyone is stable, screaming their horse name out. Thunder Snow had problems in the gate. Didn't get a good start.

The announcer begins: "2017 Kentucky Derby, Are you ready for the most exciting 2 minutes in sports" Then he continues, "They're all in the gate, and quickly, they're off. Patch's in the outside stall, Always Dreaming has a great start. Something went wrong with Thunder Snow. Classic Empire was bounced around. Fast and Accurate is there, and State of Honor has set the pace. Iraq is running 6th, Practical Joke in 7th, Gomerly in 8th, Untrapped in 10th, and Classic Empire in 13th." Around the opening turn is Givin, and it's an intense opening mile! One half mile to go. Irish War Cry and Practical Joke follow pass by Fast and Accurate. On the backstretch, State of Honor is leading, followed by Battle of Midway with Gormely close behind. On the far turn in 1st is Always Dreaming, then Irish War Cry in 2nd, McCraken swinging wide behind with Always Dreaming. Always Dreaming moved to the outside of State of Honor. He's digging down deep and holding the lead by 2 ½ lengths. Looking at Lee couldn't catch Always Dreaming. And the dream comes true! 2 minutes and 59 seconds with Always Dreaming as the winner!

Peaches Battle of Midway

Mama's → 1st Place = Always D. 3rd Place = Midway. 5th Place Practical Joke (Yussef)

Fred's → 2nd Place = Looking at Lee 4th Place (uncle Bubba) = Classic Empire

Epilogue

Following this race, everyone is trying to calm down. Mama thanked the community for showing up. They really know how to throw a derby party. This was the best party ever, Mama thought, even if she's not contacted by Tyler Perry. Instead of a reality show, Mama thought she'd like this to be a movie. Mama got a big surprise at the end of Yussef's show. Her secret admire showed up, her high school sweet heart bias. He went over grabbed her hand for a dance off BBKing song. Mama melted! And loved every moment of it.

At last, Bubba and Betty are going to continue to date long-distance. They have fallen in love! She said his baby backs were finger-licking good, and his baked beans were the bomb. Shorty said them missionary circle vegetables did him in. He was dizzy all day. He got accepted into jockey school in Minnesota, and he got a full-ride scholarship. Even though he was home-schooled until the 11th grade, his senior year was at the high school. His counselor helped him get it. We will see how that goes. He knows enough slang to get by.

In the last place, Frederick also got a 4-year scholarship for business school. He's going to Georgia Tech. She still drinks from time to time, and she is doing better with her bipolar disorder and isn't hiding it anymore. She attends monthly counseling and has been dating her secret admirer.

Fred had a long talk with Mama. She was sorry for not telling him about the bipolar disorder. He wanted to attend school in Georgia so he could check on Mama and Bubba. Melva found out she was pregnant by Fred. "Oh my!" She's no longer a jump-off! He plans to take care of his baby and be a co-parent, that is, after they do the DNA test; she might have been jumping him off. Well, he got a taste of his own medicine.

Yussef is going to continue doing comedy and coaching Little League baseball in Detroit. He plans to visit the Cuban Missile, Aroldis Chapman, during the off season. He had never in his lifetime seen a

Derby party like this before. He plans to use some of the material for his up-coming shows.

After all, Shorty was so glad his dad, Mr. Father Ruben (A.K.A. The Party Crasher), an Amish priest and Mama's neighbor, was out of town, He calls the cops every year on Mama, claiming Mama is disturbing the peace. He also claims to pray and do Bible study 3 times a week, so he needs peace and quiet.

Mama knows the whole police department, so when they arrive, she has their to-go plates ready. They party for 30 minutes then go on to their next beat. Their favorite food is Mama's braised coon with sweet potatoes; nobody in this town can cook a coon like Mama! Mama had a big smile. Everyone starts settling down; everyone grabs a second plate of food. Shorty's is stacked high with spicy Cuban wings. He's gonna regret that later! Bia is grinning from ear to ear while helping Mama. Maybe Tylrer Perry will show up at the Comedy Show!

Yussef Comedy Introduction

Fred sees Yussef and asks, "Cuz! Are you ready for these wild seniors?" His voice dropped to a baritone, and Yussef says, "I'm ready, bruh! I just got rid of those demons." "How, cuz?" "I went out to the truck and smoked a joint. I'm lit!" Fred tells him, "Just don't look at Bubba. He will become a heckler." Yussef smiled and said, "Ok, I'm cool as a cucumber!"

Yussef grew up in Athens, Georgia back in the 80's. Some already know him from childhood. He's 34 years old, and have 2 children. Yadira (10 yrs. old) and Yoenis (6 yrs. old) He's single and on the market. He's not sure if he will ever retire from comedy. A former Minor League, baseball player. Who currently lives in Detroit, Michigan. The Motor City.

He's been a comedian for years, starting in school as class clown. He's also an impersonator, has done talent shows and plays. He's a 3 time finalist at the Stardome in Georgia. He's made appearances on the HBO Stand-up Comedy Show in the 1990's.

His long term dream is to do voice acting. And he's performed all along the 120 East/West Corridor. From Texas to Florence South Carolina. Guaranteed to have you crying from laughing. Some have even split their pants. Let's welcome Yussef to the stage. They heard a sudden bang! And pop behind the stage.

It's Shorty playing Yussef's Introduction Song: My Imagination by Gladys Knight and the pips. The crowd is old and boisterous, loving his song choice. Yussef is dancing, 6 feet tall and thin as a rake.

He's wearing his flared checker board bell bottoms, black big collar button down shirt, grey clog shoes, and his big black Afro Wig, sprayed with lots of Afro sheen. He also have long hairy-side burns, which brings out his chocolate dark skin, and gap in his front teeth. His walking cane and stool "is on stage." He has a few butterflies in his stomach. His inner voice is saying, Thank God for these food choices because I was on empty until 2 hours before the show. I was sweating bullets, but I think I'm on track right now.

Chapter 6

Everyone is yelling and clapping as Yussef says, "Thanks for the heartfelt welcome. I love this job. I get to meet people from all walks of life. Y'all folks here keep it 100. Y'all got the whole liquor store up in here, legal and illegal! I didn't know y'all get down like that. I got to step up my game. They all laughed.

He continues, "I've seen a lot of beer bellies since I've been here. I can't hang around too long, or I might get one!" Gilberto laughed so hard from the crowd, and he yelled something in Spanish.

"Raise your hands if you want to attend a live Kentucky Derby race," Yussef said then asked, "Have you heard about the horse poop problems? Especially after the race. It doesn't matter, rain or shine, rich or poor, the color of your skin. You're still gonna smell poop all day long. When it rains, there's muddy poop. The horses gallop and leave droppings everywhere. They don't care! That's y'all's problem. And y'all making all that noise causes them to poop even more! You eat a barbeque sandwich, and you still smell poop. There's big hats, sundresses, suits, millionaires smoking cigars, trainers and owners, and guess what! They all still smell poop!" The crowd laughed softly.

Yussef continues, "Did you know they get rid of 30 tractor truckloads of manure and urine? Some go to local famers, some to mushroom farms. It's been a problem since 2002, and they want to cut costs because revenue has declined since 2012 to $3.8 billion. Really! But wait! They just spent $70 million on a 143-year-old track. Then it sits, empty, the rest of the year. Hey! Somebody is smoking weed, or they lacing it with the poop!" The crowd laughed so hard.

"Wait!" Yussef said, I have more. They complaining about cutting the poop cost on some stinky, smelly, rotten, spoiled poop! And the yearly revenue is $900 million! Shoot the moon! They need to let me rock that stadium after May!" Everyone laughed, and he said, "Florida-Georgia Line would be the head liner! Moving right along! How many seniors you know have been banned from a Taco Bell?

Well, it's a senior from your hometown." Bubba could feel that heat coming on. He wanted Yussef to cross the line. Yussef kept on, saying, "If you keep burning up ribs and grills for functions, you might be a serial grill killer!" The crowd died laughing! Bubba threw popcorn and peanuts at Yussef telling him, "Bugg off!"" Yussef told him, "Bye Felicia!"

"Fast and Accurate was my derby pick," Yussef admitted, telling them, "He reminds me of my baseball career behind the plate. And the Cuban Missile, Aroldis Chapman of the New York Yankees. His 105 fast ball broke a record! It was very fast, and I was accurate catching it in the Netherlands where we met. My nickname was 'Smoke.' I smoked a lot of them trying to steal bases on me. We became great friends, and I helped him defect. I was the mystery car driver! Haha!" Uncle Bubba stood up and shouted, "Stop all that lying. You lie Like a Tombstone Shorty and the audience fell out their chairs laughing, but Yussef kept on rolling like nothing happened, continuing his routine, ""Who all get these 'Robo Calls?' Scam Likely, Nuisance Likely, Telemarketer, Student Loans. They call all day long, and you can't get rid of them. I got tired of a ADAM-CHORDO, and you always know it's them because their whole name is in capital letters. So Adam called my phone, saying, Hello! This is Adam from U.S. Medical Supplies. I need more info to process your knee and back brace.' Ok, dude! Hold on a minute' - I let 2 seconds pass- I'm back, Adam. Look, sucker! Y'all acting like some bullies and thugs. Y'all fake and shady! Stop throwing shade. Who told you I needed some braces? How did you even get my number? You and your coworkers, JANET FREEST and CARLOS PINO gonna need a neck brace when I get finished "The crowd laughed unstoppable!

"Next!" Yussef goes on, "I got y'all's name on my caller I.D. Y'all called my phone 20 times last week. I got y'all's phone wire tapped and a private detective investigating. Your whole clan is about to go down. Y'all done opened up a can of hornet's nest!" Pure silence on the phone. ADAM is speechless. ADAM, are you still there? Kiss my bass! It sounded like an alien. Bubba had a blank look, but the rest of the crowd was all on the floor, laughing. Rodney whispered to Shorty, "This fool is crazy for real" Yussef closed it out.

Saturday night on stage again, Yussef was inquisitive about the names of these food selections. He said, "Y'all a community of crazy folks! This is more like a block party, but I got to address some of these. Please be patient with me." This is Lila's favorite part. She knows what type of comedian Yussef is, on many levels. She was his High School Crush.

Mama was happy Yussef stayed in town. She was really enjoying his shows, they are taking her party to another level.

Yussef had much more time to prepare for tonight. Now that he's aware of the community, he has much more material that's on fire and hilarious. He's been thinking, "I should do more shows for seniors. They're a good crowd, and they add a lot of diversity – something I've been missing out on.

Yussef Address Some Food Selections

Comedy Show
Yussef Mystery Discoveries on Mama's Buffet Table
Saturday Evening:

1.) <u>Lazy Wife Salisbury Steak</u> = Hommie! You need to divorce her. Asap!

2.) <u>Derby Brownies</u> =Ugh! What's in these brownies? Everyone looked surprised!

3.) <u>Derby Pie</u> = Double chocolate, super chewy and a unidentified ingredient.

4.) <u>Mild High Pound Cake</u> = The only high I want is my weed.

5.) <u>Beer Garitias</u> = "This the kick-off! No Mexican beer in the cocktail? Imma move on!

6.) <u>Mint Julep</u> = Oh snaps? This is on point! Just the way I like it. Yesss!

7.) <u>Kentucky Mimosa</u> = Not enough Bourbon or sage, real dry, and on my black list!

8.) <u>Dream Bars</u> = Mama I thought you stop making dream bars? She shouted! Boy bye!

9.) <u>Shell Horse Yeast Rolls</u> = How much yeast? These are gigantic and sticky.

10.) <u>Dirty Rice</u> =I hate dirty, rice, cops, women, hands, and church folks. That explain my dirty issues.

11.) <u>Porcupine Meat Balls</u> = Are the quills out? They ain't even social bruh.

12.) <u>Felicia's Mac & Cheese</u> =Yo! Felicia! I'm mad, you burnt the bottom of this mac & cheese. Bet you was on the phone. She said, "A sorry sight!" They laughed

13.) <u>Kisspie</u> = This for my girlfriend, she always spice it up! Hahaha!

14.) <u>Kentucky Coconut Pie</u> =Look's very fancy, but tasteless where's my coconut? Wanda said, stop Smoking weed! Yussef replied sit down big Mama! This is my show!

15.) <u>Coppens Penny Salad</u>="A crack head" stole the copper out this salad. Jerry popped up, I thought the copper would be safe! Yussef said, seriously!

16.) <u>Mystery Salad</u>=This whole community's a mystery cuzz!

17.) <u>Aunt-Bay-Bays BBQ Sauce</u> = Aye! Don't bring no Bay-Bay kids up in here, keep them rascal's at home, and your sauce too. They cried laughing!

18.) <u>Date Pie</u> = Uhhh! Ann I got to date you for some pie? Yep! My pie is better than the million dollar pie. She put them big bulging eyes on him. He said nah! You look jail bait, moving on cuzz! The crowd gathered themselves.

19.) <u>Fruity Green Smoothie</u> = Too many Jalapano pepper's, my tongue is sizzling, where's the fruit? Bubba said, up your behind. Yussef tripped on the mic. cord. The crowd was explosive.

20.) <u>Cuban Hash/Black Beans</u> = Aroldis Chapman. AKA (Cuban Missile) hired an Uber driver from Florida to dropped these at Mama's. Chapman wanted to turn-up the heat. I'm scared of his heat. I knew he would come through! It's a wrap!

21.) <u>Bubba's Crab Aspic</u> = Oh! Test him for crabs, Bubba shouted, rubber neck!

22.) <u>Decandet Mud Pie</u> = Wait! This all they left me? Where's my inheritance, legacy and land? Bubba shouted "Curiosity killed the cat!" Hahaha.

23.) Three Hour Salad = Carlos! What's in the salad? It's teeny-tiny beet. Been simmering for 3 hours. Couldn't get it through the border. Yeah! Right

24.) Wendy City Mexican Corn = Yo Bubba! Lock your corn down it's blowing all over Georgia bruh! Daisy said, Bubba steaming hot get a life creep!

25.) Whisky Chicken = Stop getting these chicken's drunk. Yussef was rattled.

26.) Chicken In A Package = You'll's buying chicken at the package store? How you'll getting away with this? Ask Bubba! Nah! I'm good.

27.) Chicken On The Run =Carlos, blasted out. I've been trying to catch it. This one jumped off Bubba's grill, and is running wild in the community.

28.) Grilled Chicken Backs = A cheapskate brought these, 5 pack's for $2.00. Where the meat at? That back bone pulled my filling out. Lucky stood up, I'm on social security and a $1 budget. So Yussef, zip it up! Ok! Yikes!

29.) Russian Chicken =Bruh! This ain't no chicken. The wing is the size of a Buzzard Wing. It looked hairy and creepy. You'll gonna kill someone up in here. Now, this brought the house down. They were crying laughing.

30.) Chicken Salad With A Flare = What kinda flare? Ughhhh! Rick Flair in the house? Woah! Woah! Tell your limo driver too come on in gonna be a long night. Yussef's been trying to get a 20 min. break. The crowd wants him to keep going.

31.) Sticky Chicken = Crisp, cool, and crunchy just the way I like it bruh! LOL! lf you got sticky finger's don't touch it.

32.) Stuffed Hog Maw's = Shorty! How you eat these? Cut up, put hot sauce, and throw down, I heard you don't eat these during the summer months. Shorty said, we eat everything on the pig year round. Yussef said, Oh dear!!!

33.) <u>Knock-Me-Out-Naked Bars</u> = I wanna get naked after this show with my Georgia Peach. Fred hollered! Turn-up!

34.) <u>Peaches Chicken Feet</u> = Why the feet still look limp? I thought they were supposed to be smoky? She screamed, "A leopard can't change its spots!" Dang!

35.) <u>Cregg's Pig Feet</u>= Gee whiz! These burnt to a crisp. Should've left these at home. You and Bubba been hanging out huh! Nah fool! Me and your Georgia Peach. I love them big legs she got Yussef laughed it off.

36.) <u>Blackbery and Gin Slushie</u> = This taste like moonshine, I need the recipe.

37.) <u>The Anything Goes" Pasta Salad</u> = Not me! No possum in my salad. You'll eat too much possum here.

38.) <u>Uncle Rains Gospel Chicken</u> = Who saved and baptized it? Who gave this chicken a right hand of fellowship? The audience looked misled.

39.) <u>Foundation Cake</u> = What kinda foundation? This cake collapsed in the oven. It was fed up. Hola!

40.) <u>First Lady's Spinich Dip</u> = Which first lady? Bro. they hard to find, some run their mouth too much. Rev. Woods stood up! You-you-you talking about my wife? "If the shoe fit wear it." Go lay hands on her, and you too. Rev, was dismayed. The crowd was speechless. It's after 7:30 pm Fred throws up a gang sign so Yussef could take his 20 min break. The crowd is going crazy laughing.

41.) <u>Bishops Cake</u> = Put an usher on his cake, he's known to loose his religion. The crowd nearly died laughing. As he tripped on his long black robe, and his 24-karat gold chain got lost.

42.) <u>Glorified Rice</u> = You'll got me twisted, I ain't glorifying nobody but God!

43.) Cathedral Windows = I'm scared of a window named Cathedral. Sounds deadly.

44.) Priest Lunch= Yo priest! I got your lunch! Yelp! Just like I thought undercover. "Pride cometh before a fall." Boom!

45.) Missionary Circles = Please give them a G.P.S., It's been 3 hours of circles. They still in the parking lot. The crowd was baffled.

46.) Bible School Punch = You'll drink too much, when is communion? Sis. Mae said, Uhhh! It's been 3 years ago. Yussef is open-mouthed. ughhh! Go next door and get the Priest.

47.) Baptist Pound Cake = Been waiting on this cake, where's the fried chicken and sweet tea? These 3 items is historic. Hahaha!

48.) 99 Cookies = #99 NY-Yankees (RE) Aaron Judge (AKA) "The Judge", had cookies and his Jersey Air lifted to mama's house. "So all rise up in here!" Yussef was jarred! Mama got some pull.

49.) Million Dollar Cake= A rich cake like this? I want the million cuzz!

50.) Druken Cake- Ayee! Somebody was drunk making this cake. The 3 cup's sugar is missing, it's oily and too much white lightening, but I'm lit!

51.) Hornet Nest Cake = Who provoked it and put in the oven? Peache's said, they got drunk and destroyed the hive, then cooked it. Yussef said! Oh! Snaps! Yussef returns to the stage enthusiastic, eager, and excited.

52.) Rum Cake= I'm drinking rum & coke, where's the cake? All gone cuz!

53.) Crows Nest Pie = Somebody! Anybody! This pie ain't done, it's still screeching. Peaches said, "Look before you leep." Yussef is burning hot. I did sis! Plus who stole one of the Dignified Priest Crows?

54.) Dishpan Cookies = Dang! Too much dish soap. There gushy, gooey, scummy and tragic. Fred booed him, Yussef retaliated. Get them Crows outta the dish pan they drowning.

55.) Spider Cake = A black widow OR jumping spider? Stanley answered, my wife made that cake fool, Yussef looked shell shocked and drank water.

56.) 100 Wink Cookies = Let a cookie wink at me! It's "ride or die!"

57.) Preacher's Cake = How he get a cake? He need a watch. We done had 6 closings, took up offerings and he still ain't finished. They were hilarious.

58.) Covent Pie = Ugh! Cover up pie! Where's the monks, nuns, religious brothers, and priest? Don't judge me bruh! I've been baptized 8 times, dipped in the lake 4 times and gave too many offerings. They burst into laughter. No one owned the pie!

59.) Lightening Cake =Who messing with lightening? Ugh! "Lightening Danced Across The Sky", they were thunder struck. Yussef hollered! Help!

60.) 100 Cookies = I'm done counting, just counted 99 cookies that belong to Aaron Judge. Bubba shouted! You idiot!

61.) Cemetary Cake = Mama! You still digging graves? Take this back to the cemetary. Mama snapped! He dropped the mic, low crawled under the stage chair laughing uncontrollably with the crowd.

62.) Civil War Fruit Cake = This tasted razor and rubbery. That's why my palate felt dry & itchy. Bubba shouted sit down Sponge Bob. Stop lying! Yussef wanted to destroy Bubba, but laughed it off.

63.) Chocolate Prune Cake = Very discombobulated on every side. Somebody need to be arrested. Please don't pass gas in here.

64.) Aggression Cookies = Cuzz! Don't roll up on me, "you'll don't know me from a can of paint." They were tickle pink.

65.) Pinch Cake = No pinching, cut a slice, sit down somewhere! Ouch!

66.) Grasshopper Pie = They live in the meadows! How did you keep the 2 antennae's in the pie? This a horse party, you'll got the wrong email.

67.) <u>Rhonda's VCR Cake</u> = Did it record the race? Old folk's get rid of these VCR's. Rhonda shouted! We keeping VCR's and flip phones. Bye! Bye!

68.) <u>Put Mama To Bed Long Island Tea</u> =How many times you'll gonna put Mama to bed? Victoria staggered to the stage. Mama ain't drunk, she's refueled now bounce! He wanted to go postal, but reframed.

69.) <u>Peach Vodka</u>= Yes, "This was on and popping!" Put me in a daze thinking about my Georgia Peach. Fred says, "I've seen this movie a thousand times." Yikes!

70.) <u>John Minary's Tranquilizer</u> = Nah! I'm good! My weed is my "Tranquilizer."

71.) <u>Texas Tumble Weed</u>= This won't make it in the Windy City. It will blow all over Chicago and become "a thing of the past"! Hahaha! The Weed Capital!

72.) <u>Felicia's No Name Punch</u> = Felicia! Name this punch. Is this a moonshine blend? She shouted! Yep! With plenty of basil. He said Huh! With a curious look

73.) <u>Daiquiri Fruit Salad</u> = No thanks, "I'm still tipsy from last night bruh!"

74.) <u>Open House Punch</u>= Aye! Realtor, you showing the house? Who gave him a drink? Somebody wake him up, "Seize The Day!" Hahaha.

75.) <u>One Step Lasagna</u> = You'll know I'm on a cane. Put this with the Texas 2 step slaw. Too many steps for me cuzz. See ya!

76.) <u>Instant Russian Tea</u> = Was this tea tested? Did it go through T.S.A.?

77.) <u>Georgia Peach Bourbon</u> = Brought this for my baby! My smoking hot Georgia peach. You'll feel me? Bubba said, I don't feel nothing creep.

78.) <u>Butts Gator Tail</u>= Penny popped up, Florida in the house. Go Gators!

79.) <u>Texas 2 Step Slaw</u> = Slow this slaw down, it's doing more than 2 steps. Where did the boots, belt buckle, and cowboy hat come from?

80.) <u>Tailgate Chicken Dip</u> = Leave these chickens alone, I'm still trying to catch Bubba's "Chicken on The Run"! They all giggled.

81.) <u>Bleaks Roll Tide Salad</u> =You'll ain't rolling in Georgia. Bleak your salad turned out to be Scandalous. Bleak replied, "Roll tide fool! Yussef replied "War Eagle! Now, roll that dogg. The crowd did a belly laugh.

82.) <u>Buck Eyes (From Ohio)</u> = Them deer eyes on that back table not buck eyes? Wild! So, what you'll doing in Georgia? You'll in the Big 12 Hommie! Jonta shouted! Shut up! Mama invited us. Okay! I feel you.

83.) <u>Mississippi River Mudd Cake</u>= Good grief! What's in the mud cake? Chocolate taste bulky and gooey, it's sticking to my palate, it's flaky!

84.) <u>Tennessee Sin Dip</u>= Still sinning huh? Wait a minute, I hear music to my ears. Country music playing on a guitar Nah! It can't be true, ughh! <u>Chris Stapleton in the house</u>. And he's playing, <u>Tennessee Whiskey</u>," This goes well with the sin dip. The crowd was mystified. Mama was in a daze.

85.) <u>Bubba Wallace Race Day Pie</u> = Ahem! How did we get 2 Bubba's in the house? You'll seen me in Nascar: I'm from Mobil Alabama so "Roll Tide Roll! They were all baffled, wondering how Mama pulled this off? She stood up tall and said, "Knowledge is power!"

86.) <u>Elephant Stew</u> = Keep your stew in Alabama. It's been cooking since I've been here 3 days ago. It's disturbing!

-Yussef threw up a gang sign for Fred. Look man it's midnight, when do these people sleep? OK! Let's close it out and meet again on Sunday night. Yussef said, that mud cake is doing a number on me cuz! Bye! Bye! Ohhh. I gatta address this famous SLAM! (Prison Food)

Yussef said, was that a SLAM I seen on the table? Who brings that to a Kentucky Derby party? I know exactly what that is, prison food. Ate too many growing up. My dad's favorite food. My Dad Eugene stayed in and out of prison. When he came home this all I ate. So somebody get that slam and throw it away. Never in my life wanna see another one. I was traumatized!

Mr. Eugene stood up! Boy! You always running your mouth. Ughhh! Dad is that you? I'll get back with you later. Eugene said, shut up! Opps! you'lls got me in trouble, but how could I overlook that Slam dish? Pop's I can't believe you're still eating Prison food. Ughhh! How long have you been out bruhhh? Fred turned down the Mic on Yussef, He Kept talking after 5 min. he decided to move on.

Sunday Evening:

- Yussef is back to the drawing board. What will he come up with next? Look's like this gonna be a long night.

87.) <u>Watergate Cake</u>: Who dug up President Nixon from the dead? Take this to the White House. Let President Trump cut the first piece. "Heh heh"

88.) <u>Judge Peter's Pudding</u>= Dang! Another judge? Heard this pudding was defiant and disgusting. LOL! Maybe he stirred it with his gavel. "Whatever!"

89.) <u>Govenor's Casserole</u> = Cuz! What you got going on? You went crazy with them poppy seeds. Did you measure them? They look spookish and eerie. Governor said, "Save yourself boo!" Raphael couldn't stop laughing.

90.) <u>Sardine Casserole</u> = Where's the warning sign? Eat this and get your colon cleanse for free in 30 minutes, Yussef said, "Seriously!"

91.) <u>Congo Squares</u> = Where's the drums and pretty African women? These squares are very detailed and delicious. Fix me a too go plate.

92.) <u>Republican's Pie</u> = You'll don't want no pie! Last time I checked on Capital Hill Republicans was the Crips and Democrats was the bloods and MS-13 Gang's is the Liberals. So, you'll gone and eat that pie. Rev. Al Sharpener said, sit your crazy butt down. Huh! Now that was a gut check, it took the whole house down. Hahaha!

93.) <u>Funeral Mashed Potatoes</u> = You'll got the wrong funeral home dogg! "Ohhhh!" Valdez gave me this address. Where is Valdez? Ahhhhh! You have such a good sense of humor. Yussef replied, Bye Felicia!

94.) <u>Pastor Petes Enchiladas</u> = He's in the kitchen without his armorbearer? Aah! I inspected them and they look gruesom- struck, falling apart like something outta a thriller movie. The audience were falling outta chairs laughing. Yussef split his pants in the rear, Bubba passed gas and dismantled the crowd again. Fred said, this brought down 2 houses, go Yussef!

95.) <u>Queen Elizabeth Cake</u> = Mama Fay's the only queen in here. Fred shouted! "That's my Mama "The Jack of all Trades."

96.) <u>Chocolate Prune Cake</u> = Whatcha thinking? This is an Intimidation Cake. Very dangerous combination together, chocolate and prunes? Really! Really! Really!

97.) <u>Lace Cookies</u> = Who's lacing all the cookies? Legal and illegal. You'll smoking more than young folks, ain't nobody got that much arthritis. I bet all of you'll got 2 or 3 cannabis cards. T.J. stood up! "I got my card!" And I have 2 that I sleep with at all times. Pedro spluttered, Shut up!

98.) <u>Angel Hair Pasta in Garlic Sauce</u> = Woah! Anita! "Pump your brakes!" Put something on yo! Head. Hair net, do rag, scarf, OR skull cap. Too much hair in this pasta. Red, blonde, black, blue, and gray. The little puppy Stella wouldn't eat it. You couldn't fool her. "Screw you Yussef."

99.) <u>Molded Beet Salad</u> = Yussef said, Yulk! Little Ray jumped up and said, I'mma take my molded beets, beer, and Billy Club. Gatta! Bounce bruh! Bye, bye.

100.) <u>Cream Field Peas</u> = Shorty said, "Keep it southern." Kathy said, Cow Peas, Henry said, nah! Purple Hull Peas, Jackie said, Queen

Anne been picking them all my life. Yussef looked confused, Bubba Wallace stated in Mobil we call them pink eye OR cow peas. Henry said, Bruhhh! We get down on our peas and butter beans in Bama Roll Tide!

101.) <u>Field Peas With Sausage</u> = Rick Flair went Woah! Woah! Very flavorsome, fancy and fresh. Gatta take some home cuzz! Yussef was joyous. Rick said, all you'll Ladies meet me on Space mountain after the show Woah!

102.) <u>Company Chicken Casserole</u> = Look! A chicken scandal is going on in this town. I don't want to see another chicken, casserole, nor company. Don't visit me, I'm jittery right now. Hahaha!

103.) <u>Earth Quake Cake</u> = Stale, distasteful, and outrageousness elastic. It was damaging going down my throat. But, on the other hand it looked moist and delicious. Bubba shouted! What a Bird Brain!

104.) <u>Reindeer Droppings</u> = Who brought a reindeer up in here? What a musty smell, no horse or deer droppings for me. Put this next to the deer eyes.

105.) <u>Garbage Dip</u> = Who put this in the garbage? I went right in and recovered it. It was breath tasting, bonafide, and splendid. I got down on this bruh!

106.) <u>Taco Bread</u> =Ummm! Fernando what happened to the chipotle and cilantro? Where's the heat hommie? Fernando said, Right here SA.

107.) <u>Felicia's Cornbread Pie</u> = Another pie huh! This one fell apart in my mouth, and the rubbery taste is scandalous. That was those little dropping's you hate. "Huh" Oh no! Somebody help! He dropped the mic, and started wiping his mouth. They were crying laughing for 15 minutes.

108.) <u>Walking Tacos</u> = Yo! I didn't see these on the table. Shorty said, they went on a 3 mile walk blockhead.

109.) <u>Lane Cake</u> = 2 or 3 lanes? Seniors, the millennial generation has taken over. You'll's moving too slow, Pastor Lee said, someone get me a bucket of water so I can baptize him. Sis. Sheryl said, baptize his potty mouth first. Yussef said, Sit down you'll ate too much of sin dip. Pastor said! Whatever!

NOTE: Yussef said well crowd that's all for tonight. I will see you'll tomorrow night for the finale. Same place, same time. Duces!!

Monday Night Finale

110.) <u>Gee Gee's Stew</u> = This is eye-popping, I tasted some rabbit and quail. I tasted a few feathers and felt weird. Something wasn't right, this black pepper got my tongue on fire. What kinda recipe is this? She shouted! "Straight Outta Montana". Yussef had a bleak smile.

111.) <u>Italian Collards</u>= I eat mine southern with ham hocks. These kinda gritty. I didn't know you'll ate collards. Tell the mafia to stay off my trail. Do I look like I'm from Sicily? They laughed softly.

112.) <u>Delicious Grilled Goat</u> = Shorty! This ain't delicious, I heard it screaming on the grill. Did it ever die Cuz? Yussef I'm used to it, it's called a slow death on charcoal. What! You sound like the undertaker. Nah! I'm good.

113.) <u>Cherokee Casserole</u> = Let them Indians in dawg! They rain danced the whole weekend. When did they made a casserole? Luke said, we cook at night, Yussef said Aww!

114.) <u>Football Sunday Chili</u> = Shorty you brought this? Nah! I'm drunk and high off this Texas tumble weed. I got the munchies ask Tank. Who's Tank? Fred said, no one knows him. They all looked surprised.

115.) <u>Detox Soup</u> = Dr. Green said, Take this home and drink it. Therefore we won't have to call in 5 OR 6 plumbers. Yussef said, Yike's!

116.) <u>Frito Mess</u>= Manny! Clean up your mess. Look! Hommie you got the wrong guy. That's Felix Mess. Well, it better happen before I leave this stage. Uncle Bubba said, Boo, Boo, get off the stage. Yussef shouted! Go home you Shenanigan, Bubba cursed him out. They laughed.

117.) <u>Route 66 Diner Philly Chicken</u> = Yo! Ain't no route 66 on my G.P.S., I need some land marks. Done been up and down the interstate. It's a wrap!

118.) <u>Mama's Quick Drop Peach Cobbler</u>= Mama! What you sipping on? You ain't never dropped no cobbler. They have put her to, bed 6 times, somebody bring me a shot of southern comfort. Someone said, Turn-up! Sip on this green MoonShine, Made Outta Muscadines. It's the Fire!

119.) <u>Moon Shine Apple Pie Cocktail</u> = I need to meet with you'll in the man cave. Tell me about recipes and stories. I might join you'll group. Hahaha!

120.) <u>Flips Family Potato Salad</u> = Tell Flip and his whole family. That potato salad is staggering like a drunk person. You'll's got too much of Jim Beam. We know where Flip's recipe came from the underground!

121.) <u>Drunken Cake</u> = Mr. Undercover Cop! Arrest all these drunk cakes put hand cuffs on them. Fred! Dropped the camera laughing.

122.) <u>Witche's Brew</u> = Nah! Not me! I went up in the woods, found me some home brew. Been sipping on this for 4 days. It has a nice kick bruh!

123.) <u>Tomato Soup Cake</u> = You'll did road kill on this cake, I plead the 5th.

124.) Redeye Gravy = I don't need this, my eyes stay red boo boo!

125.) <u>Feud Cake</u> = I'mma get you'll on Family Fued. I got a feud with that "going away cake" Whatcha trying to say? Mama said, "Hit dog will holler!"

126.) <u>Millionaire Candy</u> = We got millionaire's in here? Where's the candy? I didn't see any on the table. LOL! It's only for celebrities. Whatcha mean? All 4 of them threw candy at Yussef! He had a vacant look!

127.) <u>Tequila-Key (Meringue) Lime Lie</u> = Felix shouted! No more drinks for you. I'mma take that pie home cuz! Keep your "cotton candy words!" Yussef felt powerless but kept on rolling.

128.) <u>Beer-in-the-Rear Chicken</u>= Penelope slipped me this note on my break. I can't believe we have this last chicken here. Uncle Bubba stop abusing chickens, they don't like you. Bubba shouted, I'mma stick this one in your rear on the way home. The crowd was out of control laughing.

129.) <u>Kings Tavern Sweet Potatoes</u> - These came from a tavern? What? All kinds of liquor in these. I tasted that Jack Daniels. It had a kick, glad I was on my break. Haha!

130.) <u>Diabetic Hamburger Stew</u> = Huh! Everyone in here is a diabetic. Testing 1, 2, mic check! You'll's need to check your sugar.

131.) <u>Chocolate Sin Pudding</u> = Pastor Low! We see why you disappeared. You ate the whole dessert, and you tried to help baptize me. Come on up here to the stage, I need to slap a gallon of oil on your forehead. They couldn't stop laughing, Fred dropped his phone in the oil.

132.) <u>Crazy Dolly's Hot Cheese Spread</u> = I knew something was wrong with this spread. I couldn't pick it up. See I can't do crazy. Dolly stood up and said, you don't need no Georgia Peach." I'm right here bruh!" I wanna knock your boots." Yussef turned as white as a ghost; with a blank look. He gathered himself and said, go rent a room. Bring belts, handcuffs, and toys. The crowd didn't know what to do, they knew this was the end of the show because "her lovely voice was music to his ears."

133.) <u>Life Recipe</u> = This will save your life.

134.) <u>Happiness Recipe Happy Wife</u> = Happy Life.

135.) <u>Grand Finale</u> =I've been waiting all night for this cuzz! Yussef broadcast over the mic! If you're banned from Taco Bell raise your hand! Bubba tried to Mace Yussef from the crowd.

<u>Yussef's Close Out</u> = Thanks for coming out and supporting me. I've never done a 3 day comic event. This is one tough town with gritty people, At times you were frightening and furious. My bravery kicked in at times and made it blissful. You'll made me better and a lunatic at sessions.

I'm hoping this comedy will help Mama get her reality show/movie. I say good bye! Shorty blast the music with his favorite song: GHETTO WOMAN by: BB King. Yussef threw up his peace Sign! I don't ever want to see these Shenanigans again. I'mma need me a Jar of that Moonshine to take back to the motor city so we Can turn-up!

Fred threw up a gang sign to Yussef, asking him if he needs a break. No one was paying attention to it; they wanted more from Yussef. He said, "Next time, let me know what kinda people gonna be up-in-here. Y'all got everybody like Bishops, Missionaries, under-cover Priests; Gospel chicken, what that taste like? Y'all got Republicans, Cubans, Russians, goats, gada's, elephants, Montana, Moonshiners, Baptists, Sin, Decadents, and a lot of other stuff I can't mention. He's having problems closing out.

But one last thing- this is my 15th closing. Uncle Bubba! What happened to your 3 grilled chicken on the run? We seen it running on the side of the road. Right before your grill fire and explosion." Now, that took the house down! Bubba said, "Get lost, creep! Go back to Detroit!" Everyone was laughing except Bubba. He had fire coming out of his ears. "Ok! My time is up," Yussef closed, "Hope y'all enjoyed the show." Bubba took the 'going away cake and put it in Yussef's hand. Fred says, Everyone is scrambling for the right spot. Betty and Bubba are still wooing each other. Fred's puppy is playing with Peaches' teeth. Shorty gave them to her, she was so thrilled. His rear is still on fire from that jalapeno pudding. They keep watching the race over and over. Yussef is walking around talking to everyone, thinking where did these people come from?

Larry said, "Somebody turned up the heat on that Cuban hash, and I'm feeling it." Lila said, "That grilled goat was a little tough," and she's wondering if that was actually goat because she heard screaming all night. The man cave is filled with men again, all talking about the food and horses. Lars said, "That Mock Cooters stew and chicken feet was on point." Gilberto liked the BBQ grilled goat; it was peppery and gingery, like he likes his women.

Derwood said, "I'm Catholic, but that Baptist pound cake changed my religion! I'm feeling drunk off moonshine apple cocktail, and I can't remember my horses' name. Ya'll wake me up when it's over."

The ladies are in the family room, playing some Tina Turner music, like What's Love Got to do with it? Marlene slipped on a banana peel, so Shorty helped her up and put her in the recliner. She's been sipping that Knock Out punch since noon. They all loved that Kentucky Nut pie. Shorty said, "It's already a lot of nuts in here." Haha!

Fred was supposed to be filming and recording everything, but Shorty has to take over since he's talking to his ex-girlfriend in the driveway, Fred came back, saying, "Thanks, Shorty!" He replied, "Yo! I thought you and Melva broke up!" "We did, man. I told you, she was just my jump-off." Confused, Shorty asked, "What does that mean? I've never heard you use that word before." Fred told him, "It means I can hit it and quit it whenever I want." "Huh?" Shorty questioned, "Hit what? Fred told him, exasperated, "I'll explain it to you next week. This ain't the time to be giving you a one-on-one class. I got to keep this video going" "Eew!" Everyone is stationary, ready for the muddy race. The rain has slacked up, and the sun is shining bright in Kentucky. They're parading to their posts. The jockeys get to show their horses off. The 'My Old Kentucky' song has played. The horses hate that song. Big screen's everywhere for the recorded races. Ten times total. Fred said, you all have watched the derby 5 night straight . Maybe when Yussef leave, no more partying, no more facers. Go home, see you next year. Fred announced. Yussef affirmed NAH! Can't do more. Shows here, I'm going into hiding in North Carolina. Yussef stated, "Elvis has left the building."

A Few Poems To Read

"Bullet Proof"

I used to run through my hood
Thinking I was bullet proof?
Angry as hell…, temper…
Going through the roof!
I didn't give a care
About any of you,
That's until I got shot
Right on my family's stoop.
It was retaliation from a rival gang.
Cause I was at the top of the game,
Getting money, slanging them thangs.
They couldn't touch me then,
The slick thief in the night,
Or so I thought, you see…
Was leading a double life,
Filled with pain and misery.
It wasn't the fortune of the fame,
But, the thrill of it all, in and of itself…
Never knowing that the hunter…
Could very possibly..get captured…
By the game.
I didn't know that I could get touched,
By someone claiming to be my friend,
But, I know now,
As my life's blood flows,
That not every fight I can win.
I cheated death at this time,
And now I'm trying to change.
Now I fall on my knees daily,
Calling on Jesus' name.
My 5yr. old son, Chase perished,
On the mean streets of Chicago
So, now my soul cries out…
Forgive me Lord,

I'll go wherever you say go.
I hurt everyday at the mention
Of his name.
Now, as I recall my pain-filled-past,
I can truly say, I'm free at last.
No more hustling days for me,
Now I can truly say,
Whom the father sets free,
Is free, indeed.
No more Bullet Proof for me

By: ***Millie R. Lee***

"I'm A Little Different"

I'm a little different,
This is true...
I'm a human being,
Just like you.
Sometimes, I move fast,
Sometimes, I move slow...
But, it doesn't mean that I can't learn
The right way to go.
Sometimes I get excited...
Because I can't understand,
But don't give up on me...
Hold my hand, comfort me...
Love me any way that you can.
Don't get angry or start to cry,
Because it's no one's fault,
That my emotions are trapped
Within my body.
It's not easy for me to deal
With all of my emotions...
At the same time...
It scares me, too!
But, I need your help, mommy and daddy,
To show me what to do.
Be patient, be loving,
Be understanding towards me...
Don't let the enemy seep in...
Causing you to abuse me!
God will guide you, mommy,
And give you strength enough
To go on...
So, don't give up on me...
Please be strong.
I'm a little different,
Yes, this is true...

But, one thing is for certain…
I will always love you.
God loves me and you, too.
He'll give you the strength,
To see us both through.

I hope you like it! ☺
By: Millie R. Lee

Mama Share's Some of Her Recipes from the Derby Partie

Confederate Cornbread

1 cup cornmeal	¼ cup of all-purpose flour
2 ½ teaspoons baking powder	¾ teaspoon salt
¼ teaspoon baking soda	1 cup butter
3 tablespoons melted butter	1 egg, lightly beaten
1 ½ teaspoons vegetable oil	

Yield: 6 to 8 servings

Pre-heat the oven to 425 °F. In a bowl, combine all the ingredients except the vegetable oil. Grease a 10-inch cast-iron skillet with the vegetable oil and heat it on top of the stove until it is very hot. Pour the batter into the hot skillet and bake for 15 to 20 minutes.

Mile High Pound Cake

4 cups all-purpose flour	1 teaspoon baking powder
4 cups sugar	¼ cup lemon juice
½ teaspoon salt	2 cups butter, room temperature
10 large eggs, room temperature	

Dense, moist, and over-the-top good!

Pre-heat the oven to 325°F. Grease and lightly flour bottom of tube pan. Sift together flour, baking powder, and salt. Cream the butter. Gradually add sugar, beating all the time. Beat in eggs, 1 at a time. Add the dry ingredients. Beat. Add the lemon juice. Pour batter into prepared pan. Bake for 1 hour and 25 minutes, or until done. Cool on a wire rack.

Fruity Green Smoothie

1 ripe banana, sliced and frozen	1 pear, chopped
2 cups fresh spinach (or kale)	½ cup plain Greek Yogurt
1 cup almond milk	1 tablespoon honey

Makes about 2 cups

In the container of a blender, process together all ingredients until smooth. Serve immediately.

Texas Two-Step Slaw

Salad:

4 cups shredded green cabbage	1 cup shredded red cabbage
¼ cup chopped red onion	2 jalapeño chiles, seeded, finely chopped
1 (11 oz.) can vacuum-packed whole kernel corn with red and green peppers, drained	2 tablespoons chopped fresh cilantro
	1 cup shredded cheddar springs
	Fresh cilantro sprigs

Dressing:
1 tablespoon fresh lime juice
1 teaspoon cumin
¾ cup purchased ranch salad dressing

Yield: 8 (1-cup) servings

Enjoy Tex-Mex flavor with this colorfully zesty coleslaw sure to win the favor of kids and adults alike. Cheddar cheese, corn, and jalapeño chiles make an ordinary slaw extraordinary.

In a large bowl, combine all salad ingredients except cilantro sprigs; mix well in a small bowl, combine all dressing ingredients; blend well. Pour over salad; toss to coat. Serve immediately or refrigerate until serving time. Garnish with cilantro sprigs.

Dream Bars

1 stick butter	½ teaspoon baking powder
½ cup brown sugar	1 teaspoon vanilla
1 cup flour	1 cup coconut
2 eggs	1 cup nuts, chopped
1 cup sugar	1 tablespoons butter
2 tablespoons flour	2 tablespoons lemon juice
¼ teaspoon salt	1 cup confectioners' sugar

Combine stick of butter, brown sugar, and 1 cup of flour. Press mixture into 9x13-inch Pyrex dish. Bake at 350°F for 15 minutes. Combine remaining ingredients except butter, lemon juice, and confectioners' sugar. Spread mixture all over crust. Bake for 30 minutes more. Cool slightly and top with mixture of butter, lemon juice, and confectioners' sugar. Cut into squares.

Watergate Cake

Cake Ingredients:

1 box white cake mix	1 cup oil
1 package instant pistachio pudding	1 cup lemon lime soda
3 eggs	½ chopped pecans
½ cup sweetened, shredded coconut	

Frosting Ingredients:

2 (3 oz) enveloped Dream Whim	1 ½ cups milk
1 package instant pistachio pudding	½ cup chopped pecans
½ cup sweetened, shredded coconut	

Watergate Cake: pistachio, coconut and pudding in a delicious layer cake!

In a large mixer bowl at medium speed, add cake mix, oil, pudding eggs, and soda. Fold in chopped pecans and coconut. Pour into greases and floured 9-inch round baking pans and bake in a 350° oven for 35-40 minutes. Cool completely on wire rack. To frost, whip Dream Whip and milk until peaks. Gradually add the pudding and beat until light and fluffy, about two minutes. Spread on first layer of cake. Top with second cake layer and cover cake completely in frosting. Press pecans and coconut into cake and refrigerate two hours or more. Serve cold!

Kentucky Coconut Pie

1 9-inch pie shell	½ teaspoon vanilla
2 eggs, beaten	½ teaspoon butter flavoring
1 ¼ cups sugar	½ cup of milk
1 ⅓ tablespoons flour	3 ½ -ounce can flaked coconut
¼ cup melted margarine	

Mix sugar and flour together. Add mixture to beaten eggs. Add the remaining ingredients to the sugar, flour, egg mixture, and mix well. Bake pie shell about 10 minutes at 450°. Put filling in shell, reduce heat to 325°. Cook about 35-40 minutes.

Mississippi Sin Dip

8 oz. cream cheese (room temperature)	2 cups grated sharp cheddar
1 ½ cups sour cream	4 oz. chopped green chiles
½ cup chopped green onions	"fat" French loaf
8 oz. Bryan canned ham (not spam)	corn chips

Combine all ingredients besides loaf and chips Fill French loaf with dip. Bake at 350° for 1 hour, uncovered. Serve with corn chips and enjoy!

Derby Brownies

½ cup butter, softened	½ tsp. almond extract
1 cup sugar	¼ cup butter, softened
4 eggs	2 cups sifted powdered sugar
1 cup all-purpose flour	2 ½ tbsp.. Green crème de menthe
¼ tsp. salt	16 oz. pkg. semi-sweet chocolate morsels
1 ¼ cup chopped pecans	¼ cup butter

Yield: 4 dozen brownies

Cream ½ cup softened butter; gradually add sugar, beating well at medium speed. Add eggs, one at a time, beating after each addition. Combine flour and salt; add to creamed mixture alternately with chocolate syrup, beginning and ending with flour mixture. Stir in pecans and almond extract. Spoon batter into a greased and floured 13 x 9 x 2 inch pan. Bake at 350° for 25 minutes or until a wooden pick inserted in center comes out clean; beat at medium speed until mixture is smooth. Spread over brownie layer. Combine chocolate morsels and ¼ cup butter in top of a double boiler; bring water to a boil. Reduce heat to low; cook until chocolate melts. Spread over frosting. Cover and chill at least 1 hour.

Bacon and Bourbon Collards

4 thick slices of bacon	1 tsp. dried crushed red pepper
3 tbsp. butter	6 lb. fresh collard greens, trimmed and chopped
1 large sweet onion, diced	½ cup apple cider vinegar
1 12 oz. bottle of beer	1 tsp. table salt
½ cup firmly packed brown sugar	½ tsp. freshly ground black pepper
½ cup bourbon	

Yield: 10 servings

Bourbon, bacon, and beer give collards a rich and earthly flavor. The vinegar added at the end gives a zip to a hearty cold-weather side dish.

Cut bacon crosswise into ¼ inch strips. Melt butter in a large Dutch oven over medium heat; add bacon, and cook, stirring often, 8 minutes or until crisp. Drain bacon on paper towels, reserving drippings in a skillet. Sauté onion in hot drippings 3 minutes or until mixture is reduced by ¼. Add collards, in batches, and cook, stirring occasionally, 5 minutes or until wilted. Reduce heat to medium-low; cover and cook 1 hour or to desired degree of doneness. Stir in vinegar, salt, and pepper.

Mississippi River Mud Cake

Cake:	Frosting:
1 cup butter	1/3 cup
2 cups granulated sugar	½ cup butter
4 eggs	½ tsp vanilla extract
¼ cup cocoa powder	⅛ tsp salt
¾ tsp salt	1/3 cup light cream or milk
1 ½ cups all-purpose flour	1 16 oz. box confectioners' sugar
1 tsp vanilla extract	
1 ½ cups chopped nuts (pecans preferred)	
1 9 oz. jar of marshmallow cream	

Yield: 12 servings

Cream butter and sugar in a large mixing bowl. Beat eggs, one at a time. Sift cocoa, salt, and flour, then add to egg mixture. Stir in vanilla coconut, and chopped nuts. Pour batter into a greased and floured 13 x 9 x 2 inch pan. Bake in a 350° oven for 30 to 35 minutes, or until toothpick inserted in center comes out clean. Remove from the oven and, while hot, spread with marshmallow cream. Let cake cool then frost with frosting.

For frosting: Beat cocoa, butter, vanilla, salt, cream, and confectioners' sugar in a medium mixing bowl until fluffy. Spread over marshmallow cream on the cake.

Texas Tumble Weeds

½ cup sugar	1 cup orange juice
6 large fresh sage leaves	1/3 cup bourbon
1 ¼ cups club soda	(substitute for extra orange juice for a virgin drink)

Stir together sugar and ½ cup water in a small saucepan over medium heat. Bring to a boil, and cook, stirring occasionally, 3 minutes or until sugar is dissolved. Remove from heat; add sage leaves and let stand for 5 minutes. Remove sage leaves. Stir together syrup, club soda, orange juice, and bourbon in a large pitcher; add ice cubes to fill. Serve immediately.

Copper Penny Salad

2 lbs. Carrots, peeled and sliced	¾ cup vinegar
1 med. Green bell pepper, diced	1 tsp prepared mustard
3 med. Onions, sliced into rings	1 tsp Worcestershire sauce
1 can cream of tomato soup	Salt
½ cup salad oil	Pepper
¾ cup sugar	

Yield: 6 servings

Cook carrots until tender but not soft. Place cooked carrots in a large bowl with bell pepper and onions in layers, sprinkling each layer with salt and pepper. Mix soup, sugar, salad oil, vinegar, mustard, and Worcestershire sauce together and pour over vegetables. Cover tightly to refrigerate for 12 hours before serving. Drain portion of dressing from vegetables. Then serve as a vegetable or a salad on lettuce. (Left over dressing may be used on tossed salad.)

This Tee Shirt belongs to Tanner.

Uncle Bubbas Ribb's!!!

The chicken on the run been jumped off the grill, It's somewhere in the community running around.

Uncle Bubba's Ribs before the explosive grill fire,
and the Mexican Street Grill Corn.

These are the Ribs that blew up in the front yard and the birds are having a feast. Buzzards, Crows, Indian Vulture and the Red Tail Hawk.

Betty's Baked Bean's

Felicia's Yankee Birthday Cake At A Horse Party!!!

Bubba's Saying's in his Kitchen

Derby Food's

Derby Food's

Derby Food's

Derby Food's

www.ingramcontent.com/pod-product-compliance
Lightning Source LLC
Chambersburg PA
CBHW030306130626
46549CB00002B/723